# The Deep State Prophecy and the Last Trump

**Kenneth B. Klein**

**El Dorado Publishing - Folsom, CA**

The Deep State Prophecy and the Last Trump


Cover Design by Connie Treantafeles
Interior design by El Dorado Publishing

ISBN: 978-1-947165-79-3



Printed in the United States of America.

What happens when the dark side of the spiritual realm
overshadows the political world...

# Contents

# Introduction

## The Global Cauldron

Has there ever been a time in history quite like this? The world is experiencing a great convolution as never before. Each day there is another major crisis. It is unprecedented!

Certainly, the Fukushima nuclear disaster tops the list threatening the wellbeing of the oceans. Then, there are major geological disasters of hurricanes, earthquakes, and massive fires breaking out upon the earth. In addition to the threat of nuclear war there is the threat of electromagnetic pulse weapons. A global economic collapse with the world's massive indebtedness is just around the corner. And, to put a cherry on top, we have the terrible reality of global terrorism.

But within the United States, the disturbing problems are not just external, and these problems are most noticeable with the youth. They are the most disturbing symptoms of a culture gone askew.

The problem is not just confined to the youth. Over the past fifty years, there has come a noticeable dumbing down of the overall populace from top to bottom. There has come an evisceration of common sense.

The plague of ignorance is not just with the United States. The same is true of England, France, Germany, and all of Europe, as well as many other parts of the world. Unfortunately ignorance becomes the lens through which people view the world. And that lens is clouded over.

This book is about medicine. It is the antidote and prescription for staying the plague. It is about the restoration, if not for the soul of a nation, at least the restored mind of individual men and women.

It is a gathering of missing pieces to a puzzle extracted from the annals of time. It is a crystal clear picture painted from the heavens, an eye salve for healing smoked-filled eyes and the restoration of faraway vision.

# Preface

There are times when men should be unafraid to shake up their thinking. Why do we do what we do? Why do we think what we think? For some, this could be an intimidating exercise. It has been said, "Whatever can be shaken will be shaken." But if we are really standing on solid ground, we should fearlessly embrace the challenge. After all, who wants to build on quicksand?

The teachings presented in this book challenge the fundamental Christian worldview and, on a grander scale, call into serious question today's prevailing biblical eschatological (prophetic) point of view.

The initial launching pad is the premise that there has never been a clear guidance system for the interpretation of the book of Revelation. The Christian community has had only vague understanding of John's Revelation, because the context of the Revelation has never been pinpointed with clear biblical clarity. Once the context has been grasped, then sound interpretation can follow. Herein lies the clarity.

**The Context**

First, the letter is from Him who is, who was, and who is to come (Revelation 1:4). God, who is, dwells in the realm of eternity; therefore He is.

He was, meaning He, Jesus, was amongst men when He died (on the tree). He is to come; He will return to this time dimension at His Second Coming.

We see the explanation of God's existence from the point of view as from heaven to earth.

He is, He was, He is to come. We also see that the letter was written from the presence of the seven spirits before the throne of God. The context of the writing is heaven and eternity. (The seven spirits are another mystery to be revealed at another time). Second, He is the Alpha and the Omega (Revelation 1:8), or the beginning and the end. This verse speaks of time as God knows time. God, who is, has neither beginning nor end. He is from the beginning of creation until the end of time when the universe folds up as a scroll. In other words, God is outside of time, and He sees into time from the end to the beginning and from the beginning to the end all at once.

In order for us to wrap our minds around the true meaning of the symbols of Revelation, we must begin by grasping the context of the writings of Revelation. The context is written from outside of time as we know and understand time.

This is an enormous problem. Our minds naturally operate within the context of human time. We are programmed to think and conceptualize within the context of historical human time. In the book of Revelation, we are faced with the task of trying to understand matters from outside of time—from God's point of view. If we do not begin with this premise, we tend to force a linear progression and materialization of application (an earthly meaning) on the symbols before we understand their spiritual nature and meaning.

Third, John says, "I was in the spirit on the Lord's day" (Revelation 1:10). Does anyone really know what this means?

This problem becomes more prominently evidenced in modern teachings. Revelation 1:19 says, "Write the things which thou hast seen, and the things which are, and the things which shall be hereafter." Immediately it is assumed that this means past, present, and future as pertaining to Earth time.

The theologians force the interpretation into an earthly linear time sequence. But the context is not Earth time. It is heaven time. John is seeing these things in the spirit, not foremost on the earth. The sequences of the heavenly events are just that: in the heavens.

The book of Revelation is about spiritual codes that were written in symbolic form or symbolic language and unfolded in a certain sequence: Things that he has already seen, things that he is about to see, and things that he will see in the "spirit." Most of our thinking about Revelation has been misconstrued and placed into an Earth time linear chronology.

Since all appropriate biblical exegesis utilize the principle of time (the eternal Word was spoken in time), history is an essential element for interpretation of Scripture. The book of Revelation has, for the most part, no earthly historical context. It is written from a heavenly perspective.

Man's problem in attempting to interpret the Revelation is that he is trapped in a human time prison, causing him to apply a sequential historical (earthly) perspective.

A proper context is the key to understanding the most mystical book ever written. It was written from God's point of view, God's context, outside of time as we know time.

# Chapter One

## The Enigma of the Last Trump

Was it a serendipitous coincidence, unexplainable happenstance, anomaly? It is easy to overlook the obvious elements of a spectacular event and miss minute, but very significant, details hiding in the background. Such was the case in the more than classic intrusion that overtook one of the most important personages and events in human history.

On his way to destroy Jewish people in Damascus who had decided to embrace Jesus, the super-religious zealot, Saul of Tarsus, was intercepted by Jesus Himself.

A blinding intense light shone round about Saul and effectively and totally blinded him. In a kind of incredulous stupor, he asked, "who art thou Lord?" Give him some credit, at least he recognized it was God. "I am Jesus," of course in the true vernacular He would have said, "I am Jehu, or Yeshua. Why do you persecute me?" (Acts 9:4-5)

Cut to a man named Ananias, a believer in Christ who was also visited by God and was instructed to go to this man, Saul, and lay hands on him and pray that he may regain his sight. Reluctantly, because of the evil reputation of Saul, Ananias obeyed.

But, and this is the point, what is missed in the pinnacle moment in time is a very critical detail. Contained within the specific instruction is a pinpointed location for where Ananias was to go. "Go to a street called Straight!"

This directive with such specificity to a precise location must be underscored in our minds, because it is somehow lost or at least obscured from notice.

Again, would this be irony, serendipity, anomaly or just plain coincidence?

It is almost humorous. Yet here at the street called "Straight", Saul gained not only his physical sight but his internal sight. It is at the street called Straight where Saul, who later became the apostle Paul, for the first time in his life began to see straight.

What an incredible underscoring of the conversion event. Other than Jesus, including the apostle Peter, no one had greater influence on humanity in all of human history than Paul. He wrote half of the New Testament. His conversion was epic, and where did he regain and then gain his sight? At a street called Straight.

The Almighty God orchestrated the events, even to the smallest detail, of where the monumental event would take place. It was to underscore for all time what happened to Paul and at a place that bespeaks what happened to him.

God, in His great love for humanity, goes to extraordinary lengths to make His person and His plan to be made known to mankind.

**The Last Trump**

One of the most mystical, enigmatic, and widely debated and discussed passages in all scripture is the term at "the last trump." The portion of scripture where this term is found is in the book of 1Corinthians, and pertains to the monumental event when at the last trump, all who are followers of Christ will be instantaneously transformed into a different type of body.

This historically unprecedented yet future event takes place at the last trump. Where the trump takes place and how it takes place is for now just academic conjecture. But with so much talk circulating in light of worldwide growing political tensions, looming ecological calamities, threats of wars, along with massive radiation leaks into our oceans, many wonder if we are not in the last days of mankind.

In light of all these matters, what is so fascinating about the signal of the last trump is that it becomes serendipitous in conjunction with the name of our current president, Donald Trump.

Could this once again be the Great God our Father orchestrating events to underscore what He is doing and about to do in the heavens? Might Donald Trump be His underscoring of a dimension we are not able to perceive?

**The Great Mental Disease**

July 21, 2017. Two boys stand at the shore and observe a feeble man struggling for help. The man seems to be drowning. The boys continue to watch, but instead of rushing into the waters they begin to chuckle under their breath. Their quiet laughter turns to outright back-slapping hysterics. Finally, the helpless man goes under and drowns.

A man driving in a dark sedan drives by a lake shore.

Suddenly from out of the passenger window, a burlap bag flies into the frigid lake waters. A woman driving behind the dark sedan stops and wades into the water and rescues three puppies tied up inside the bag.

Are these just isolated instances of callous and heartless indifferences. or are they symptoms of a growing trend of a broader national and global sickness? What are we witnessing? What is happening to humanity?

**Suddenly-A New President?**

All of a sudden almost without rational explanation a business man without any political experience inexplicably was an elected president. When all the polls showed otherwise Donald J. Trump was miraculously elected into the highest office in America and arguably the most powerful office in all the world. The pundits were stunned. The world was in utter disbelief. How did this happen? How could this have happened? He came out of nowhere. He was considered a joke.

Yet here was the new American president. Almost immediately, a relentless media attack ensued. From the offices of legal jurisprudence, federal judges, attorneys, and congressmen in both House and the Senate join the rebellion.

Inside his own administration, classified information was leaked to the news media. Even within the FBI, CIA, and NSA, there surfaced tremendous pushback. How was this growing divisive and massive opposition to be explained?

Was it the man, the office? Who was Donald Trump? Perhaps a better question what is Donald Trump, just another president? Or was he somehow ironically connected mysteriously with the last trump that sounds at the end? And what was Donald Trump trumpeting causing this great derision and acrimony? What was

Donald Trump pointing to that was creating the great uproar? Whether he knew it or not he had become a major irritant and annoyance to the New World Order, or as the scripture calls it the Beast.

**The Deep State**

Donald Trump, more than any president in history, was endeavoring to overthrow and defeat the "deep state." "Drain the swamp" was the motto. But the depth of the deep state is deeper than one can imagine. It is far more than what can be presently observed on the surface. It is deeply entwined and embedded in the fabric of our mighty nation. It is a terrible cancer and a sign not to be ignored. The shroud of darkness coming over America as well as the whole world, has been developing for many centuries.

So we should ask ourselves could it be that in God's love for mankind, He sent Donald Trump as a great trumpet to shed light on what the prophets had warned of two thousand years ago? Are we to dismiss this underscoring which may be a prophetic statement, and a sign that we are nearing the last trump of the transfiguration? Is Trump a Godsend that is providing a reprieve?

Is God trying to underscore what is at hand in similar fashion as Paul's supernatural event at the street called Straight?

Neither Abraham Lincoln nor John Kennedy, both assassinated for their attempt to stop the New World Order in their day, can equate to Donald Trump's effort to drain the swamp, which is the deep state. In biblical terms, the deep state is identified as the Beast and the False Prophet of the apocalypse.

**The Depth of the Deep State**

How deep is the deep state? Draining the swamp is not

merely skimming off the scum on top of a disgusting pond.

One could associate pond scum as the thousands of political operatives within the Washington D.C. beltway, but that would be a only superficial understanding of the swamp. The swamp that Trump, is at war with is a very deep swamp.

# Chapter Two

## The Lord's Day and the Swamp

In the first century the apostle John was able to perceive in symbolic form, the deep state while he was in the spirit on the Lord's Day.

The meaning of the Lord's Day and the Sabbath is the entry point and may best be understood in the following light.

The Lord's Day is the true Sabbath Day, but it is not the Sabbath that has been traditionally or historically understood and kept, nor what people in general believe.

In the era of the Old Testament, the Sabbath Day was understood as from sundown Friday to sundown Saturday. In the New Testament times, it was changed to Sunday. The Jews and other religions, keep it as Saturday. Nevertheless, it was and still is kept as a specific day to commemorate and remember the seventh day of creation.

On that seventh day, the Lord rested from all His labor. The Sabbath was the Lord's Day, but the Sabbath that John was keeping on the isle of Patmos was not Friday sundown to

Saturday sundown. It was different. It was not a specific day.

The book of Hebrews explains and gives a different understanding for the Sabbath. It describes to the people of God they had still yet a Sabbath to enter into. The book of Hebrews uses the example of Joshua in the Old Testament to set the stage for explaining the concept for the proper keeping and proper meaning of the Sabbath. Here is what it says.

> "Now if Joshua had given them rest, God would not have spoken later about another day. So there remains a Sabbath rest for the people of God, for whoever enters God's rest also rests from his own work, just as God did from His." (Heb 4:8-10)

In other words, Joshua, upon taking them out of the wilderness and into the land still did not give God's people rest. Likewise, the proper Sabbath is not about a day of the week, but rather about hearing God's voice. So we find that the Sabbath is today.

> "So today, if you hear His voice, harden not your heart." (Heb 3:15)

When we hear God's voice, we enter the Sabbath day rest. The day of the Lord is the Sabbath day and John knew how to enter the Sabbath day rest. This was a different kind of Sabbath than what had been commonly and previously observed. It was not a specific day like a Friday or Saturday or a Sunday. The Sabbath day is today.

**Adam and Eve**

The creation of Adam and Eve was on the Sabbath day.

When God rested on the seventh day, He still managed to create Adam and Eve, and He also planted a garden. The garden was, of course, the garden of Eden. So where was His resting?

He rested from the first six days which were conceptual days of creation.

**A Great Metaphor**

Just as a movie begins with a script and is the conceptual stage for movie making, so too were the first six days (yoms) of creation. So then the first six days of creation were the scriptwriting stage and not the actual physical materialization. After the sixth day God rested from the script. Then on the seventh day He created or manifested mankind in the flesh. We see God making Adam in the flesh, and also planting the Garden of Eden on the seventh day. (Genesis 2:5-8)

**Examining the Third Day**

The perfect proof and evidence for this fact is by examining the third day. On the third day, God conceptualized plants, but these conceptual plans for plants preceded the conceptualization for the sun. The sun was conceptualized on the fourth day. (Genesis 1:11)

How could there be plants without the necessary element of sunlight?

Yet we find on the seventh day there were no plants. If plants were created on the third day how was it there were no plants on the seventh day? Where did the third day plants go?

The answer is that the first six days of creation were the conceptual stage, not the actual physical stage of the materialization of creation. It was not until the seventh day that the actualization or the materialization of plants and everything else, including man and woman took place.

## The Analogy of Creation

A perfect illustration of Genesis is to understand the distinction between the initial conceptual planning work (the first six days or yoms) of creation from the following physical manifestation of creation which was the seventh yom.

Just as a movie first exists on paper as in a manuscript and is the conceptual creation, so was the rendering of creation explained in the book of Genesis. The first six days of creation was the scriptwriting stage, so to speak. It was followed by the seventh day which was the manifestation of the first six days of planning.

When the author of a film finishes the writing down of his idea, he then rests from the writing stage, it is then time to do the filming of the movie with cameras, actresses, and actors, sets and so on.

Just as there cannot be a house without first the blueprints and there can be no movie without a script, there could be no creation without first a plan.

The first six days were the planning stage of creation. But please note the literal Masoretic text.

> "And Elohim blessed the seventh day and sanctified it because that in it he had rested from His work which Elohim created to make." (Genesis 2:3)

## The True Sabbath Rest

It is interesting that every one of the six days of conceptualization of creation ends with the words the evening and the morning." Those words are more accurately rendered as setting and the dawning, but it was not the setting and then dawning of a twenty-four hour day. It was the setting and the dawning of an age.

In other words they had an ending and a beginning. But on the seventh day/age when He rested from the conceptual writing stage, there are no words morning and evening i.e. setting and the dawning. That seems to indicate that there is no beginning nor ending to the seventh day. The Lord's Day has no beginning nor ending. It is a perpetual day and a perpetual rest, and that is why the book of Hebrews says the Sabbath is today.

> "So there remains a Sabbath day rest for the people of God. For whoever enters God's rest also rests from his own work, just as God did from His." Ibid.

John knew how to perpetually enter the Sabbath day rest, which is perpetual and every day. He did not write the book of Revelation in one session, but he knew how to enter the Sabbath day rest, which is today.

Paul must have known as well. He speaks of a man (himself) who was caught up; whether he was in the body or not he couldn't say (2 Corinthians 10:2). He was lifted out of time, as was John when he received the book of Revelation.

Peter also may have been able to tell us of the Sabbath day. He fell into a trance while sitting on a rooftop and saw a sheet descending with unclean animals. "What I have cleansed no longer treat as unclean." But the Lord's command—"Arise, Peter, kill and eat"—had nothing to do with eating unclean animals.

It had to do with how God was accepting the Gentiles. The symbol of the sheet and the unclean animals had nothing to do with the tangible eating of unclean flesh as Peter initially thought. It was about a spiritual matter. Salvation was being opened up to the Gentiles.

When Peter, James, and John accompanied Jesus to the

Mount of Transfiguration, they were transported into the realm of the spirit and became terrified. Yet they had been introduced into the Lord's Day. Notice what they said.

> "Let us make three tabernacles, Lord; one for you, one for Moses, and one for Elijah." (Matt.17:4)

They were trying to bring their spiritual experience into an earthly time context. This is exactly the problem with our approach to the book of Revelation. We try to re-contextualize the book according to time as we know it. Getting outside of time is by achieving the Sabbath day rest. The Sabbath day is the Lord's Day.

What follows is a presentation of the effect of the unseen world, expressed in symbols, breaking upon the physical creation. Now that we have some semblance of finding the way outside of human time by entering the Sabbath day rest of the seventh day, we are going back to Earth to begin to observe how the spiritual contained in symbolic format manifests on Earth.

# Chapter Three

## The Secret Rendevous

In a large office sequestered in a small English town, a man sits in front of an enormous but primitive computer system. With his headphones on, he strains to listen. The year is 1941. The town, Bletchley Park. The office is British counterintelligence for Europe. The computer is the newly constructed cipher system, used for eavesdropping on the German military broadcasts. The German code: the Enigma.

Over the past number of years, television's History Channel has effectively reported on some of the greatest secrets of World War II. England's brilliant decrypting technology via the invention of the computer cipher was the most important weapon of the allies in World War II. The brain trust that created the cipher was the greatest assembly of talent during the war. Although Germany had suspicions they were being spied on, they never figured it out.

Hitler and the German high command did not believe it was possible that the Enigma code could be cracked. It was much too complicated. Nonetheless, the Fuhrer took precautions by scrambling the code on a daily basis. Yet, British intelligence was still able to consistently intercept information from Hitler's Third Reich.

As a result of this tremendous advantage, the Allies were able to continuously outflank the German wolf packs (submarines) in the north Atlantic. Not only was the battle for the Atlantic successful, but the Allies' advance information continually frustrated German strategy and tactics in the land battles for Europe as well.

But then it happened. A high-ranking officer of the German military carried a bomb in a briefcase into a secret meeting with Hitler. The bomb was placed at the feet of the Fuehrer. The bomb exploded, and Hitler was seriously wounded. The assassination attempt failed. Hitler survived. The war continued. But the attempt on his life made him exceedingly paranoid. He refused to allow any war-related information to be communicated by radio. All information was now passed by couriers, who were guarded by his infamous and trusted Gestapo.

Back at Bletchley Park, message interception—and, thus, the flow of secretly deciphered information—screeched to a halt. An intelligence blackout. For the first time of America's entry into the war, the Allies were blind. They had become so dependent on the rich source of intercepted German information that the intelligence blackout meant that the greatest military blunder in world history was about to take place.

Three months after the blackout, the Allies were overly confident that Germany was defeated in that late summer of 1944. However, without their advanced upgraded information on the state of the German war planning, they were headed into a grave error. They fell into a state of optimism and complacency, falsely believing the war was coming to an end. After all, France was being liberated, and the German army was retreating back to their own borders.

But Hitler had a secret plan. "The Watch on the Rhine," a massive military counteroffensive, better known today as what would become the "Battle of the Bulge." It was a massive military operation that came seriously close to succeeding.

Heroic men saved the day, and Germany's last gasp did not succeed. Had it succeeded, Hitler would have gained atomic weaponry, and the world would be a far different place today.

What a lesson! But what can be learned from it?

Have we lost our ability to cipher prophetic events in the light of the panoramic spiritual perspective? Has a massive evil counteroffensive been launched against the world and God's kingdom? Have we too become smug and over- confident in ourselves, as were the Allied generals of World War II? Are we really aware of what is taking place, or have we become dulled down to the degree that we cannot perceive what is really happening? What has become of our objective perspective? And how does America and England fit into the end time scenario?

# Chapter Four

## Instruments of Darkness

They slipped out of New York without being seen. They changed their names and rode the lowly subways. They falsified their itinerary. In the middle of the night, they made their way to the secret meeting place.

Their rendezvous had been carefully prepared. Already, the hideaway was sealed off and guarded in strictest isolation. All English-speaking servants were released. Every possible leak of information was sealed. There was no chance for the knowledge of the event taking place to slip out. What was at hand was the final episode in the conquest of the United States of America, the event that would consummate a two-hundred-year plot to seize the hidden conduits of international capital.

This last stroke, the final blow, would effect the realization of an ancient conspiracy that would finance a new Global World Empire. The means would be the centralization and control of money.

The secret location for the meeting was a millionaire's

retreat called Jekyll Island, located off the coast of Georgia.[1] No name could have been more fitting for such a place of treachery.

The name Jekyll was immortalized by the great Scottish author, Robert Louis Stevenson, in his famous book Dr. Jekyll and Mr. Hyde. Stevenson's masterpiece tells the story of a benevolent Dr. Jekyll, who, while working in his laboratory, discovers a drug that turns him into a beast (Mr. Hyde).

Jekyll Island, a place of seclusion and tranquility owned by the rich and powerful, became a laboratory for concocting an evil scheme. The poisonous potion of the scheme, once consumed by the American republic, transformed it into a Mr. Hyde, a beast.[2]

This is the true story of six thousand years of watching and waiting for the final rebellion, characterized by the emergence of a Global World Government of promised peace and prosperity. A neo-garden of Eden; a heaven on earth.

The last two centuries have witnessed the final chiseling of an ancient historic monument—a monument erected by the corporate will of the human race. There is an inscription at the foot of the edifice revealing a fantastic testimonial: Man without God is a beast.

**The Chosen Ones**

For hundreds of years, the people of God have been anticipating a Global World Empire ruled by the Antichrist. In the 1930s and 1940s, many thought that Adolf Hitler and Benito Mussolini were the Antichrist and the False Prophet. Bible believers viewed the National Socialist German Worker's (Nazi) party as the Beast that would fulfill the prophecy of the books of Daniel and Revelation.

In the 1960s, scholars and spokesmen from Dallas Theological Seminary, and books such as Hal Lindsey's"The

Late Great Planet Earth," focused the North American church, both Protestant and Roman Catholic, on the European continent as the place where the Beast would rise with his ten horns or kings.[3]

When it became known that the European Common Market would be limited to ten nations, it seemed clear to many that those nations comprised the ten kings. It looked as though the European nations perfectly fit into the fulfillment of Daniel's and John's prophecies.

A horn in Scripture is interpreted as a king or a kingdom, so the announcement created much interest and excitement in the church world. However, now there are more than ten members of the Common Market, and after many years the excitement has waned.

As a result, many today are perplexed and confused trying to figure out how all the prophecies fit together.

The European Common Market has now grown well beyond ten nations with several Eastern European nations joining, but Scripture is clear that there will be ten kings that are submitted to the little horn, the Antichrist. During the Nixon administration, the United States was divided into ten economic zones. In addition, the Club of Rome announced that the world globe has been divided into ten federated economic regions. Which of these scenarios represents the mysterious ten kings? The fact of the matter is that the mysterious ten kings have yet to clearly materialize and be identified, but according to Scripture, they will.

But how will this come about? Who and what is driving the world toward this World Global Empire? What role did these powerful men gathered at Jekyll Island play in the formation of this anticipated Global Empire?

**The Instruments of Darkness**

From the time of man's expulsion from the Garden of Eden, history has recorded the efforts of the unseen"god of this world" and his relentless movements to consolidate and control this planet. The notion that a man can be righteous in and of himself without spiritual rebirth is the annoying, but pervasive sound played on the flute of hell's Pied Piper. For some six thousand years, the children of Adam, by and large, danced to that tune, but the music is about to end.

Through powerful spiritual forces working behind the scenes of the visible world, over the millennia man has dutifully and collectively—and blindly—worked on earth to bring about the final rebellion against God in this neo-Babylon called the New World Global Order.

There are some men, to be sure, who have taken actual oaths to the devil himself, and knowingly set themselves to do battle against God. Others have unwittingly become ensnared in the plot. But in this conflict there is no middle ground; one is either for or against the Lord. In the realm of the spirit, the battle lines have been drawn, and very soon the "Mark of the Beast" will be the line drawn in the earth. Whoever takes that mark will have lost all hope.

From Nimrod to Caesar, from Weishaupt to Hitler, and, ultimately, to the Antichrist himself, the events of history have been, and are being, orchestrated toward a One World Government and the worship of a man—the Antichrist, who will one day proclaim himself to be king of the world.

Through technology, religion, politics, and money, the world has been manipulated and duped, and we are moving ever closer to that day.

Now, as the cornerstone of the Global World Order has

been laid, the nations of the world are unaware of the terrible iron trap that is about to snap closed. Where are "the sons of light"? Where are the prophets—the Daniels, the Jonahs, the Jeremiahs? Who will declare this age?

## Chapter Five

# My Brother's Keeper

> "Except a corn of wheat fall into the ground and die, it abideth alone: but if it die, it bringeth forth much fruit." (John 12:24)

So begins one of the greatest Russian novels of all time, The Brothers Karamazov by Dostoevsky. Dostoevsky was concerned about man's conscience and his responsibility for his brother. This theme ripples throughout his book.

The question, "Am I my brother's keeper?" is best addressed in the book of Genesis.

At the dawn of history, Adam and Eve, the progenitors of the entire human race, gave birth to two sons. They named them Cain and Abel. The lives of these brothers, though real, are also symbolic in nature. They represent two great spiritual truths. A careful analysis of them will explain the forces that have worked down through time shaping the whole of human history.

## The Cain and Abel Mystery

Cain was a farmer, a tiller of the soil. Abel was a shepherd. When the time came to worship God (Genesis 4:3-4), Cain offered the fruit of the ground. Abel took one of the firstborn of his flock and slew it before the Lord. According to Scripture, Abel's offering was accepted by God while Cain's was rejected.

The question naturally arises, why did God accept Abel's offering and reject Cain's? A close inspection of each man's approach to God will reveal the role of the two principles of life which emanate from these brothers and flow like rivers through the course of human history. These principles affect the governing of the human conscience—and, therefore, affect every human being ever born. In Abel we see the "Mystery of Righteousness," in Cain the "Mystery of Iniquity."

## The Two Mysterious Trees

The Mystery of Righteousness corresponds to the tree of life, which we find in the Garden of Eden. The Mystery of Righteousness was the life of God, the tree from which man was allowed to partake of freely. The life of God is eternal life. As long as man ate of that tree, he would attain to immortality. The mystery of the garden is much deeper than that which is offered in the doctrines of traditional Christianity, but that is for another book.

In the garden, God placed another tree. This was the tree of the knowledge of good and evil. But of this tree God commanded man not to partake. This second tree created a dilemma. Through this dilemma, God established man as a sovereign entity by giving him the opportunity to exercise choice. Man could choose to continue to partake of the tree of life, or he could choose to partake of the tree of the knowledge of good and evil.

There was another consideration attached to the exercising of choice: God said regarding the tree of the knowledge of good and evil, "in the day that thou eatest thereof thou shalt surely die" (Genesis 2:17). There was a dire consequence for disobeying God's directive. Notice that the tree gave the knowledge of both good and evil, not just evil. What in actuality was this tree of the knowledge of good and evil?

The tree of the knowledge of good and evil represented the Law. In the Mosaic law, the commandment "Thou shalt not steal" (Exodus 20:15) established the fact that stealing was contrary to God's righteous nature. On the other hand, the Law also implied the opposite. To not steal, given the opportunity, is an act of that which is good.

Here is a demonstration of the knowledge of good and evil as defined by the Law. The Law separates good and evil. Eating the fruit in disobedience to God had terrible consequences. Not only did breaking God's law mean death, it meant that one was all the more bound by the Law. The rule of law when it arrived on stone tablets via Moses simply served to show how man had fallen from God and His nature.

While the life of God manifested in the "tree of life" produced righteousness, the tree of the knowledge of good and evil could not. The tree of the knowledge of good and evil was a curse: It gave knowledge of righteousness because it could divide between good and evil, but it could not produce righteousness. There was no empowerment from the tree of good and evil to perform that which is good.

The partaking of the tree of the knowledge of good and evil produced the fruit of death; hence, to this day, all men must die.

Consequently, the deadly result caused by Adam and Eve has overtaken the entire human race from the beginning of time.

At least time as we know it. All humanity has been born under the Law—under the curse of the tree of the knowledge of good and evil.

**The Mystery of Righteousness and the Tree of Life**

When Abel took a lamb and sacrificed it to God, his act of worship demonstrated a recognition and fundamental understanding of the human predicament.

Abel saw himself defiled and separated from a holy God with no means of restoration. In humility Abel came before God, acknowledging his need for cleansing and forgiveness. He recognized that it was humanly impossible to regain the former state and be released from judgment. By himself it was a hopeless predicament, and a hopeless situation. As a result of his understanding, he made his appeal to God, hoping He would be merciful.

Abel's recognition of his own fallen situation, his depravity, and hopeless condition was the key for him to make the acceptable and appropriate sacrifice.

Though the written law of the Ten Commandments did not come until the time of Moses, centuries later, Abel knew the truth, because the Law was written on his heart—as it is with all men. He recognized that his fallen nature would continually default from God's nature and His perfect standard. No matter how sincere his attempt, he was inconsistent in his efforts to conform to the righteousness of the Law. He was trapped in his fallen nature; a slave to his inability to live the Law which expressed God's divine nature. It is the same for all men.

Abel's sacrifice to God was not a representation of his own labor or ability. On the contrary, it was a representation of his recognition that no work or human effort could gain him the approval and acceptance of holy God for a restored righteousness and a relationship. God, in His mercy, accepted Abel's sacrifice because it was an offering based upon his need, not his effort.

In Abel's sacrifice we have a preview of the Messianic mission and purpose of Jesus, who is, in Himself, the sacrifice. Christ fulfilled the requirements of the Law. He was the perfect sacrifice which Abel's sacrifice foreshadowed and foretold. Christ in His mission provided another tree. It was the "Unforgettable Tree." In Christian parlance, it is called the Cross.

**Cainism**

The recognition of human iniquity comes from the knowledge of the Law, for the Law explains and defines good and evil. The greater the knowledge, the more profound the effect upon the conscience. This was Cain's irreconcilable predicament.

Cain's worship offering to God was essentially a representation of the work of his hands, his own effort. Cain sought approval and relationship with God on the basis of his own effort, or hard work. He was the embodiment of today's self-made man, or any man. We cannot fix ourselves by being good or doing good works.

Cain's understanding and hence his sacrifice represent the antithesis of Abel's, and it is characteristic of the same delusion that has always rested on all humanity. Tragically, Cain never arrived at the awareness of his untenable situation. He tried to atone by his works, and God refused his sacrifice.

Through each man's sacrificial approach to God, his thought life was radically set in motion.

Cain's approach brought rejection; hence, anger, hatred, and murder filled his heart. Abel's approach brought acceptance with God, and peace reigned in his heart and mind.

The conscience is the doorway through which thought enters the great room of consciousness. Human thought correspondingly produces behavior. Thus conscience, whether based upon proper or improper relationship with God, affects the thought life and, subsequently, either good or bad behavior. This is why the thought life needs to be grounded in sound doctrine from Scripture.

This principle of human action as the outworking of conscience not only applies to individuals singularly but also to corporate bodies, in the collective conscience of a group, or even of a nation or state. An example of this on a group level would be the vigilantism of a mob lynching. The mob, trying to right a perceived wrong, collectively commits the sin of Cain, i.e., murder. The same corporate confusion applies in a riot.

Grasping the critical lesson of the story of Cain calls for great objectivity. But if we can wrap our minds around this curious story, we can observe the impact of these principles on the whole of human history. Since the principles are dynamic, and not static, failure to grasp the importance of the story results in a vulnerability to deception by the spiritual forces that operate unseen—forces that weaken a spiritual worldview.

**Cain and the Christian Worldview**

Cainism has also weakened the Christian worldview, and this has occurred over and throughout time. Cainism has subverted the proper approach to God. In many ways and many places, it is man's approach to God on the basis of his own effort. This is religion in a collective sense, We can also see the effects of Cainism operating within our own American political system; in fact it is in every political system.

The most glaring example today is in the realm of American foreign policy on the Middle East. Cainism, couched in "humanitarianism," imposes itself on the land of Israel insisting on a doctrine and policy for a Palestinian state coexistent with Israel.

Since 1948, the official United States foreign policy concerning Israel has been in accord with the United Nations resolutions for two states: a Jewish state, Israel; and a Palestinian state, Palestine. Did they forget God? It was He that officially declared that the land was forever given to Abraham and his descendants through his son, Isaac.

This was His sovereign choice contained in the Abrahamic covenant. (Ishmael had no inheritance in the land.) Nonetheless, men have tampered with God's sovereign election of Israel and the specified land boundaries.

Man's altruistic humanitarian justice ethic is the same as Cain's. It seems very just and noble and righteous, but it is contrary to God's sovereign plan and choice. Today, not only is this the prevailing American position, but it is unfortunately shared by the United Nations. Notice the pervasive nature of Cainism.

These political machinations demonstrate human ideas that emanate from a kind of pathology that is sourced in a failure to grasp Cainism. Nonetheless, the collective wisdom of the state is not of God. It is the collective corporate wisdom of Cainism coming to the forefront in our time, and it will certainly usher in the false peace of which Christ warned—and which the world is buying into wholeheartedly.

The effects of Cainism can also be seen in contemporary religion with its focus on self-esteem. In true Christian faith, Scripture instructs man to deny himself, take up his cross, and focus on loving God and loving his neighbor—as opposed to the modern philosophies of self-discovery.

Yet, the pervasive power and self-righteous appeal of Cainism is causing great religious deception, even in the Christian Church. Many are unwittingly being set up for Cainism's crowning achievement: the Antichrist.

Some would argue that this is a harsh and inhuman attitude. But not if the cultural religious ethic is more exalted than the biblical ethic. The religious ethic, as seen in our Pledge of Allegiance ("one nation under God"), is nothing but a cliche with little or no spiritual reality. We are self-deceived into thinking we have a biblical worldview when, in actuality, we have a tainted American worldview laced with Cainism.God is not an American.

This corporate self-deception is synthesizing into global dimensions and will finally metastasize when the nations eventually establish a New Global World Order and a temporary peace. It will be the final global rerun of Cain's offering.

No matter how grand the effort—even of the magnitude of a New World Order—mankind is still left with a stained conscience. We can't escape. This isn't to say that doing good is wrong, but we must accept the fact that doing good just isn't good enough to gain approval and acceptance with God. We are still left short.

When the spirit of nationalism (the synthesis of the spirit and will of the members of the nation state) rises higher than the Spirit that exalts Christ, the state has become deified—and its people have fallen into idolatry.

Cain was egocentric in that he thought he could better himself—and his position with God—on the basis of his own effort. He failed to recognize his inherent evil nature and God's solution for his predicament. In his confusion, Cain sought, through human endeavor and achievement, to establish his own righteousness.

Abel's sacrifice, on the other hand, was not aimed to impress God; rather, it was an astute recognition of his hopeless predicament. He cast himself on God, believing God to be merciful. Thus, Abel's offering foreshadows the Messiah's death on the tree as man's only means of salvation and recovery from his precarious condition.

Herein lay the two principles that dichotomize the undercurrents of all human thought and behavior throughout human history: Since man cannot live with his guilty conscience, he either inadvertently selects Cain's approach to God or, if he recognizes his calling, he chooses Abel's approach, and humbles himself and repents.

On the surface, Cainism appears more powerful, has more appeal, and seems more righteous. This is because it caters to the ego of man, and it gives expression to man's need for purpose and meaning in this life. This type of fulfillment is a temporal avenue and does not take into account God's eternal plan for mankind. Neither does it answer the need for an eternal answer and meaning for existence.

The collective guilt of the nation, arising as a result of ignoring Abel's sacrifice, provides an open door for the emulation of Satan's lust for power as well as a reenactment of his pursuit of it. This is the driving force of the enormous effort toward the construction of the deep state's New Global World Order.

Abel's sacrifice, by prefiguring the tree (the cross) of Christ, laid down the basis for restoration with God, a clear conscience, and, therefore, the ability to partake again of the tree of life—the life of God, which is love, joy, and peace.

All of human history has been shaped by the two principles embodied in the lives of these two brothers. Cainism, with its refusal to concede to the inherent broken nature of man, strives vigorously, but futilely, for a self-adjusted righteousness through good works. Ableism represents the basis of the New Covenant, which rests on the foundation that “without shedding of blood there is no remission [forgiveness of sin]” (Hebrews 9:22).

The worldviews of the brothers are in direct collision, and their concepts of self are directly opposed. They are totally irreconcilable and can never merge. The divergent pathways that have been built on these two spiritual roots have affected the nature and expression of every human soul and nation state that has ever existed.

# Chapter Six

## The Mystery of the Mark

"And the Lord set a mark upon Cain, lest any finding him should kill him." (Genesis 4:15)

The "mark of Cain" has been a point of discussion and debate since time began. When Cain's descendants perished in the great Noahic flood, what the actual mark of Cain was has been left to speculation. There is no longer a literal mark. What has remained is the symbolic significance of Cain's mark and its new coming emergence in the "mark of the Beast."

God marked Cain because he murdered his brother Abel. Actually, the mark represented Cain's allowing sin to have mastery over him. Cain could not master sin because he thought his good hard work would balance out the scale and correct any of his wrongdoing, thus thinking his works would make him a righteous man. He never came to accept and recognize that sin was embedded in his nature.

Cain was jealous and hateful toward his brother; it was his nature. As a result, Cain slew Abel.These two men, both literally and symbolically, represent the two principles that operate the human conscience and impact human life throughout time, as we have already noted.

Abel's relationship with God is evidenced throughout history. The Law of the Jews pointed out that a blood sacrifice was required for atonement for sin. It was written into their ancient sacrificial ordinance, and today it can be evidenced in the New Testament era through the sacraments of communion. But the greatest evidence is seen when a human life is transformed by the power of God. In the future, we will see it environmentally in the millennial reign of Christ.

Cain's system can be seen and is manifested in the Gentile world governmental systems and in all religions where law is exalted. Its final form will be the Global World Government, which is called the Beast system. The Beast and all whose names are not written in the Book of Life will be marked with the neo-mark of Cain called the "mark of the Beast." It is the mark of the system.

**Neo-Cainism**

The mark of the Beast, mentioned in Revelation thirteen is the representation of the world's greatest technological economic system and religious worship incorporated into an identification mark.

The mark represents the highest corporate achievement of the human race, and it is the crowning work of mankind—the Utopia of which men have dreamed since time began, man's futile attempt to return to a Garden of Eden.

The mark identifies all who receive it as those who believe

in man, the finest, most altruistic qualities of the human being.

It is a system that exalts man and defines him as the triumph of evolution. In other words, it encompasses everything that man is and all he has done collectively, from the beginning until now, and his final effort to establish world peace and safety in fortress Earth.

This colossal effort is the last days offering of Cain once again. And once again it will be rejected by God. But all those who buy into the system—knowingly or ignorantly—will receive on their hand or forehead the neo-mark of Cain, the mark of the Beast.

**History of the Mark-the foreshadowing**

In the pre-Christian era, there was one who was given great insights into these mysteries. His name was Daniel. He was one of the four great prophets of Israel. Daniel's prophetic writing reveals insights into the mysterious mark of the Beast.

God defined the nature of Gentile world empires as animalistic. Daniel portrays them in his visions as wild beasts without God as their ruling and controlling authority (Daniel 7:1-12). For example, Daniel saw the Babylonians as a roaring lion. The Medo-Persian Empire he characterized as a bear. The Greeks he saw as a leopard with two wings. The last ruling empire was different than all the rest. The last empire he explained as a beast which had no earthly counterpart; it had ten horns and one more little horn.

The apostle John, in the first century of the modern era (some six hundred years later), also caught a vision of this last beast. His description is found in Revelation 13. Here we find a strikingly similar representation of the last great world Gentile power that Daniel described in his writings.

Curiously, we also find that this last great world Gentile power (the completed system) was actually brought to completion by another Beast, a second Beast that is described as one that had two horns and looked like a lamb but spoke like a dragon (Revelation 13:11). What was this second beast?

**The Second Beast**

This second Beast has been wondered and talked about for centuries. It is a confounding theological perplexity and a great and deep mystery. In addition to its identity, it uses principally three different abilities (powers/signs) or tools in finalizing the construction of the great first Beast system. (Revelation 13:13-18):

1. fire that comes down from heaven
2. an image that speaks and has spirit life.
3. a mark, which is 666, without which no one will be able to buy or sell.

The last of these three remarkable abilities is called the "mark of the Beast." The mark of the Beast is the most talked about feature of the supernatural abilities of this two-horned Beast.

The mark obviously relates to some kind of economic system that will do away with the previous necessities for gold, currency, or money as we have known it.

It will be an economic system unlike anything that has ever appeared anywhere in history. It will be a system in which all the world will participate—or else go without buying or selling. It will be a system without any measure of money that has ever been known (see Chapters 30-31 for details).

## Chapter Seven

# Great War in the Heavens

According to several Old Testament passages (see Ezekiel 28, Isaiah 14, and Genesis 1), prior to the creation of man, God set up His governance in the heavens with governing angelic principalities. Three of the most powerful of these entities were archangels. Their names were Michael, Gabriel, and Lucifer.

Many today, especially in the western hemisphere and the industrialized nations, regard this history as mere myth. Very little credence is given to the existence of the spiritual realm.

In these nations, utilitarianism and materialism tend to pervade the consciousness of the populace. The citizens of Western nations see very little need—nor do they place great significance on—the reality or existence of the spiritual world.

Nevertheless, Scripture records that God created spiritual beings to govern His celestial domain. The most powerful and talented of all was the archangel Lucifer. The prophet Ezekiel was given great revelational knowledge and insight into Lucifer's beauty, authority, and power (see Ezekiel 28:13-19).

Lucifer was one of God's chief assistants pertaining to a specific grouping of angels. Under his command, he also had his own vast network of subordinates that assisted him in the work of governance.

We would do well to consider this powerful position Lucifer had in God's government. But in his pride he incited a war in the heavens amongst the angels. He was thrown out of his office of the Morning Star and cast down to Earth for instigating the war.

> "Then I looked again, and I heard the voices of thousands and millions of angels." (Revelation 5:11)

This incredible description of an angel circuit, when calculated, would equal about one trillion angels. All these spiritual beings or powers were under the command of Lucifer.

These were the angelic creatures who followed after him when he was cast down to earth. So the vast array of fallen angels is quite formidable, and they have been deployed to study each and every human being, and some deployed to reign over specific geographical areas of the Earth.

Lucifer was described as the angel who covered; that is, he was established to be over this multitude. His great beauty and splendor were unparalleled, his musical talent unmatched, his intelligence incomprehensible to humans.

On Earth he uses his great abilities and talents to deceive spiritually frail humankind by an almost infinite variety of devices.

Although God in His foreknowledge recognized what troubles the future held, He entrusted Lucifer with great knowledge, insight, wisdom, and understanding into the workings of His celestial kingdom.

Prior to Lucifer's fall and the ensuing war recorded in

Revelation 12, his pride and self love was off the charts as he sought to compete for God's very rule. It was for his disloyalty and insurrection that he was cast out from his position and imprisoned on a speck of dust called Earth. What a judgment! His freedom and authority had spanned the heavens, but now he became a convict imprisoned to a tiny prison planet somewhere in space.

God's anger would not rest with this expulsion alone. Lucifer's disloyalty created a tremendous void in heaven's government. Scripture records that a third of these created beings in God's government were also cast out with him. Lucifer carried off in his rebellion one third of the angelic host under his charge (Revelation 12:4).

The enormity of this loss, in earthly terms, is comparable in modest terms to running the federal government without the United States Congress. It would be a literal impossibility.

The Lord, in His foreknowledge, wasn't taken by surprise. He had the predetermined plan of recovery and restoration.

He created and positioned mankind to take Lucifer's lost position. This added to Lucifer's judgment; he would be forced to witness his replacement being prepared and raised up right before his own eyes.

When man was conceived of on the sixth day, Lucifer's plight had already been calculated.

Then on the seventh day/age when man appeared, he began to be assailed by this enemy (Lucifer, is known on Earth as Satan) Satan immediately went to work attacking mankind whom he deceived and enticed into following after him. Over the millennium, he has continued his deceptions seeking to subjugate this world under his authority keeping mankind from his destiny.

So then, from the beginning of human history, Satan has been working to gain total control over the earth's people by setting up his own government. That governance has been characterized in symbolic language in the apocalypse as the "Beast."

Through spiritual deception he has captured human beings and harnessed them as his instruments to bring about his plan. His plan is a government where he would rule and ultimately be worshiped. Formerly, he demonstrated the same wicked insurrection when he originally sought to possess God's throne. On Earth, he is merely trying to accomplish the same thing as he continues to unfold his evil nature and character. No mere mortal has the intelligence to out think nor escape his brilliant scheming. Only after one has been enlightened by the Holy Spirit can one begin to fathom the depths of Satan.

**God is Raising up His Sons and Daughters**

God, in His majesty and foreknowledge, has intervened and interrupted Satan's attempt to destroy mankind: God sent His Son, Jesus, to rescue the human race. Nonetheless, Satan's government, as it currently gains momentum, will lead many to assume that Christ's rescue mission failed. There are even religious cults that claim this to be so, but it is far from the truth.

In the face of Satan's New Global World Order, the Messiah is calling for an elected people to follow him. These elect people, whom He calls His son's, (women included in the sonship) are called from all nations and are in the process of transformation. Their character is being refashioned after the likeness of their God and Savior, Jesus Christ. The nature of Christ must be developed within the context of a grand conflict. It is as though every son must stand face to face with a gigantic antagonist.

The process is the preparation for assuming the office of the Morning Star which was lost to Lucifer.

This is God's purpose and process as the heirs live out their lives awaiting the appearance of their true King. The contrast and conflict between these two warring entities and governments is the cosmic context, cathedral and venue for that process of transformation.

Furthermore, the saints must experience the effects of the conflict in order to fulfill their eternal destiny with Christ. They will face conflict and resistance from the forces allied with Satan's movement toward a Global World Order. This is to be expected. There can be no progress of transformation without the drama of the conflict.

The wounds inflicted in the conflict initially evidenced in Jesus' pathos are the sacred stripes or wounds whereby it is eloquently stated,

> "by His stripes ye are healed." (1 Peter 2:25)

The saints are required to resist the devil and to stand for righteousness. They are instructed to pray, "Thy kingdom come. Thy will be done in earth, as it is in heaven" They are called to "fight the good fight", and to "love not the world."

This objective perspective is vital. The subjective human predicament and the pressure from environmental forces and factors become so overwhelming that, without this objective point of view, it becomes exceedingly difficult to stand strong in faith. What a testing!

We must have the insight to know what the enemy is doing. We must understand his plan so we are able to resist his deception and maintain the vigilance of faith.

That is why it is vital to be able to perceive Lucifer/Satan's plan, over the centuries, in the construction of his New Word Order. And now in more recent times with the aid of the emergence of the second beast called the False Prophet described in common language as the deep state.

## Chapter Eight

# The Invisible

As we have previously stated, throughout Scripture, there are passages alluding to the unseen spiritual realm which was formed by God before the material realm was created. Two of the most notable passages on this subject are in Isaiah 14 and Ezekiel 28.

> "How art thou fallen from heaven, O Lucifer, son of the morning! how art thou cut down to the ground, which didst weaken the nations! For thou hast said in thine heart, I will ascend into heaven, I will exalt my throne above the stars of God: I will sit also upon the mount of the congregation, in the sides of the north: I will ascend above the heights of the clouds; I will be like the most High." (Isaiah 14:12-14)

> "Moreover, the word of the Lord came unto me, saying,

Son of man, take up a lamentation upon the king of Tyrus, and say unto him, Thus saith the Lord God; Thou sealest up the sum, full of wisdom, and perfect in beauty. Thou hast been in Eden, the garden of God; every precious stone was thy covering, the sardius, topaz, and the diamond, the beryl, the onyx, and the jasper, the sapphire, the emerald, and the carbuncle, and gold: the workmanship of thy tabrets and of thy pipes was prepared in thee in the day that thou wast created. Thou art the anointed cherub that covereth; and I have set thee so: thou wast upon the holy mountain of God; thou hast walked up and down in the midst of the stones of fire. Thou wast perfect in thy ways from the day that thou wast created, till iniquity was found in thee. By the multitude of thy merchandise they have filled the midst of thee with violence, and thou hast sinned: therefore I will cast thee as profane out of the mountain of God: and I will destroy thee, O covering cherub, from the midst of the stones of fire. Thine heart was lifted up because of thy beauty, thou hast corrupted thy wisdom by reason of thy brightness: I will cast thee to the ground, I will lay thee before kings, that they may behold thee. Thou hast defiled thy sanctuaries by the multitude of thine iniquities, by the iniquity of thy traffick; therefore will I bring forth a fire from the midst of thee, it shall devour thee, and I will bring thee to ashes upon the earth in the sight of all them that beholdeth thee. All they that know thee among the peoples shall be astonished at thee: thou shalt be a terror, and never shalt thou be any more." (Ezekiel 28:11-19)

Since the fall of Lucifer as a result of the angel wars, there have been powerful negative forces operating in this unseen spiritual realm. These forces have victimized and afflicted mankind in ways he simply cannot perceive. Satan has brilliantly organized this world into a complex system of politics, economics, philosophy, education, culture, science, and religions.

**Religious Deception**

Although Satan (Lucifer/Satan must be understood as the opposing forces) operates in every area of deception, he is especially adept at religious confusion. As stated above, he was on the mountain of God. The term mountain of God refers in Scripture to the government of God.

> "And the stone that smote the image became a great mountain, and filled the whole earth." (Daniel 2:35)

Lucifer's great understanding of the great things of God made it easy for him to arrange counterfeits of worship. These things he is able to create in codes. Once his deceptions were designed, they were poured out on the earth. It can be a designed mental disease for a specific person or a comprehensive design on a grander scale such as a religious construction. The Eastern religions, for example, are the masterpiece of religious confusion and most readily able to be seen. They are designed to deceive the multitudes of the peoples in specific parts of the world. These matters are delegated to certain chief fallen angelic principalities who spread their spiritual diseases into the multitudes.

Space does not allow for a discussion of the world's vast array of religions including some Christian groups that have also careened off the pathway of truth.

Since the discovery of the serpent in the garden, there has always been an evil executive power on Earth for the completion of the goals of darkness. The end of it all will be a global world kingdom for the man, the Antichrist himself.

Through his seductive mind-bending power to bring almost total obedience and worship to himself through a global government, most human beings will not see the results of his incredible evil brilliance. He is the master of confusion and deception, and the whole world lies in the power of the evil one. This multi-millennia process and effort is reaching its final and conclusive form.

When the millennial bug problem of the year 2000 threatened to shut down the world's computers, a massive, two-hundred-billion-dollar repair program further galvanized and streamlined the world's global computer system. That event advanced the world toward the ultimate grip of darkness and its comprehensive control over the earth, thus paving the way for the mark of the Beast. But keep in mind, the mark of the Beast system is performed not by the Beast, but by his colleague the second beast called the False Prophet.

That there is a definite strategy at work to bring this about is stated and restated throughout the Old and New Testaments. For those watching and paying attention, it is palpable and almost tangible. Nevertheless, there are few that maintain wakefulness, keeping watch of the advancement.

The strategy is clearly evidenced throughout ancient history, and it was prominently and most clearly evidenced as it surfaced in the blatant atrocities of Adolph Hitler and his Third Reich in the past century.

**Unfolding Satan's Plan**

It is not the intention here to speculate on the future but to lay out historic and current trends that are in alignment with the ancient prophetic writings. Therefore, what is being set forth is not intentionally predictive but, rather, interpretive, so that we might clearly see the hour in which we live and how we should respond and conduct ourselves.

> "And let us consider one another to provoke unto love and to good works: Not forsaking the assembling of ourselves together, as the manner of some is; but exhorting one another: and so much the more, as ye see the day approaching." (Hebrews 10:24-25)

The day of Christ is clearly approaching. We must stay attentive and awake to the many signs of our times. Jesus predicted that from the time of the destruction of the Jew's temple there would be a long intervening period of "wars and rumors of wars." "Nation would rise up against nation. There would be famines, pestilence, and earthquakes" (Matt. 24:6), and that response to his disciples has certainly happened.

And yet, He said these were not the signs of His coming but He said, " the end is not yet." These issues were only the beginning. Yet how often is it heard, to look at the increase of earthquakes and rumors of wars as though these were the signs of His coming? No! Not so! The often overlooked sign is that of the advance of the Global World Government.

**Signs by the False Prophet**

But, what did not happened until the last one hundred years or so has been the advancement of the sign and the attesting wonders of the so-called False Prophet, mentioned in the book of Revelation chapter thirteen.

Nor, until 1948, was there any possibility of the rebuilding of the Jews' destroyed temple. ("Jerusalem and the Lost Temple of the Jews" for a full explanation of the Jewish temple).

These signs are all part of the last days scenario that will overtake the inhabitants of earth. It is as though the earth is groaning, like a woman about to give birth. As we get closer to the end, these pangs will get more frequent and intense and be of greater duration. Scripture indicates that there would be specific signs to watch for, indicating the nearness of the day of the Lord. Another one of the most important of these signs is mentioned in 2 Thessalonians 2:13.

> "Let no man deceive you by any means: for that day shall not come, except there come a falling away first, and that man of sin [lawlessness] be revealed, the son of perdition." (2 Thessalonians 2:3)

There have been those who tried to force this passage, by using the Greek text, to say the word apostasia actually means a departure from the earth. The word departure, they say, is actually a reference to the Rapture, the translation of the saints mentioned in 1 Thessalonians 4:16,17. But this is an unfortunate forcing of the scripture.

The rules of interpretations, hermeneutics, call for the weight of Scripture, meaning we must also look at what the rest of Scripture says about this topic. The weight of Scripture decidedly leans toward an interpretation of the word apostasia as a departure from the faith.

**The Great Falling Away**

> "Now the Spirit speaketh expressly, that in the latter times some shall depart from the faith, giving heed to seducing spirits, and doctrines of devils." (1 Timothy 4:1)

Scripture points out that many would depart from the faith (Matthew 24). The word apostasia, used in 2 Thessalonians 2, does not indicate a Rapture reference.

The context indicates that before the day of the Lord, there will be a time of darkness (spiritual darkness) such as the world has never known.

It is the powers of darkness which cause many people to abandon their faith in Christ. In the final onslaught, the powers of the evil one will cause many to fall away and be lost.

The failure of the restraining force which, is both law and order and the Church will allow for the great falling away and enabling the Antichrist to appear. It will be what sets up Lucifer/Satan's New World Order, his kingdom on earth.

## Chapter Nine

# The Mystery Man of Iniquity

The Man of Sin will be manifest before the day of Christ. The importance of this sign is noted by Scripture, and it is one of the clearest signs of the advancing day of the Lord.

> "That ye be not soon shaken in mind, or be troubled, neither by spirit, nor by word, nor by letter as from us, as that the day of Christ is at hand. Let no man deceive you by any means: for that day shall not come, except there come a falling away first, and that man of sin [lawlessness] be revealed, the son of perdition."(2 Thess. 2:2-3)

The Church should be watching for the coming of Jesus by paying attention to the advancing of the Antichrist system and its leader, the Antichrist, notwithstanding also the False Prophet.

There are those who maintain that so long as the Church is on the Earth, the Antichrist and his associate the False Prophet cannot come forth. But they tend to forget that the Protestant Reformation which began in Germany shortly thereafter fell under the spell of Hitler. It took only three centuries to fall into such great darkness. Where was the Church to stop that Anti-Christ? Hitler was most certainly an Anti-Christ, yet where was the Church ?

As the Church becomes weaker and weaker, it will not be able to stop the Man of Sin or the man of lawlessness. It is the great falling away that permits the Anti-Christ to advance.

First of all, the government of the Anti-Christ, or the system, is called the Beast. It can be most readily observed by the advancement of the global government in the United Nations. The government precedes the man.

The Antichrist will be the commander-in-chief of the notorious Beast system that was foretold in the books of both Daniel and Revelation.

The signs of the day of the Lord were carefully pointed out to those who lived in Thessalonica. The Thessalonians were instructed to keep their eyes not only on the clouds but also on the earth as well. Jesus said,

> "And when these things begin to come to pass, then look up, and lift up your heads; for your redemption draweth nigh." ( Luke 21:28)

**Where to look**

The prophet Daniel spoke of the "people of the prince" to come as the ones who would destroy the temple of God in Jerusalem (Daniel 9:26). The Romans, led by Titus, sacked Jerusalem in AD 70, and are those designated by Daniel as the people of the prince who is to come. Here we have a clue as to where the Antichrist will come from.

Today, the present day location of the old Roman Empire is Europe, but there can be no doubt that the scepter of the influence of Rome also shadows the United States. He will be a Western man, and the location of his great kingdom will be in the area that comprised the old Roman Empire. That is because it was the Romans under Titus who, nearly two thousand years ago, began to set the stage for the coming world dictator. The Romans were the people of the prince to come to whom Daniel was referring. The prince to come is another mystery. Most students believe "the prince to come" is a reference to the Anti-christ. But is it?

The present day location of the old Roman Empire is Europe. Through the unification of the Common Market by various treaties, economic ties, and the Euro, the stage is now set for the advent of the Antichrist. But we must be mindful of the fact that it was the people of Europe that also founded the United States. America also lies in the shadow and influence of Rome. Regardless of whether "the prince to come," as mentioned in Daniel 9:26 is a reference to the actual Anti-christ or to a fallen dark angelic dignitary, there is a powerful overshadowing occult influence upon the United States.

One only has to look at the effect of the Masonic Lodge's influence in this country to see the impact over the history of the United States, and that influence originated out of Europe.

**How He will Approach**

By taking a look at the past, we can see the unfolding of foretold prophetic events. The spiritual cataclysmic event of Lucifer's mutiny and his resulting judgment—as presented in Isaiah 14, Ezekiel 28, and Revelation twelve—brings out two key thoughts:

1. Satan was cast down to weaken the nations. The weakening of the nations, as Ezekiel pointed out, was caused by the abundance of trade, or merchandising.
2. He has celestial beauty and spiritual knowledge. He corrupted these traits and uses them to deceive the world.

Beauty, or appearances, money, or mammon, and religious confusion are the instruments through which he is bringing his control over all the earth.

**Manifestations of His Agenda**

The spiritual effect of Satan's control of the world can be most easily seen in the multitude of religions worldwide. But his agenda also includes a One World Global Government, with a man of his choosing to be at the head of it.

Satan has been working for thousands of years to set up his earthly throne. Now, two thousand years after the birth of Christ, we are very near the completion of Satan's world government. Let us trace the progression of his efforts.

The most powerful political office on Earth is the presidency of the United States. Could this be an important focal point for a massive spiritual onslaught? When one stops to consider the proximity of the headquarters of the United Nations sitting on American soil in New York City, the prospects for the setup of a world government is right before our eyes. And it may very well involve the highest political office in the world; the seizure and capture of the office of the presidency of the United States.

# Chapter Ten

## City of Harlots

An understanding of Mystery Babylon's historical influence from Eden to present is imperative to achieving a greater objective understanding of Satan's work in the world.

In the book of Revelation, perhaps the most infamous language that symbolizes the worldwide religious confusion is seen in the great harlot of chapter 18 of the book of Revelation.

We find her referred to in highly symbolic language: "Mystery Babylon, the Mother of Harlots." Many have offered interpretations of this mystery woman, but by and large she is a false representation of God's true church on the earth. She goes about seducing the inhabitants of the earth through false doctrines and perverted ideas of God. (Revelation 18:1)

In both Revelation 17 and 18, we observe two features of Mystery Babylon: Mystery Babylon, Mother of Harlots; and Mystery Babylon, the Great City.

It is vital to underscore the point that Mystery Babylon Mother of Harlots, is clearly a global religious deception that operates under Satan to deceive the whole world..

Mystery Babylon, the Great City, is also the commercial industrial complex that operates in conjunction and in coordination with the pseudo-religious matrix. This satanically infused mystical industrial complex is the grist that lubricates the wheels of the foundation of the prophesied Beast system mentioned by both the prophet Daniel and the apostle John.

**The Birth of the Beast**

After the world was destroyed by the biblical flood, it was repopulated through Noah's sons, Shem, Ham, and Japheth, and their descendants. Nimrod, a descendant of Ham, began the organization of great cities, building the first great city, Babylon, in the post flood era (see Genesis 11:19).

> "And Cush begat Nimrod: he began to be a mighty one in the earth. He was a mighty hunter before the Lord: wherefore it is said, Even as Nimrod the mighty hunter before the Lord." (Genesis 10:8-9)

The expression "he was a mighty hunter before the Lord" can carry a hostile meaning. The word before is sometimes used as meaning "against" the Lord. The Jewish encyclopedia says that Nimrod made all the people rebellious against the Lord.[1] During his time, Nimrod fit the picture of the first Antichrist. There have been many antichrists, but he was the first. The Antichrist to come was predicted by the apostle Paul in his book to the Thessalonians. Yet, according to God's word to Eve, one day a deliverer would come. Scripture says:

> "And I will put enmity between thee and the woman, and between thy seed and her seed; it shall bruise thy

head, and thou shalt bruise his heel." (Genesis 3:15)

Many though, in the ancient days of Nimrod, thought Nimrod was the promised Messiah and looked to him as the savior of the world. There were many legitimate reasons why people felt that way even though they were gravely mistaken.

He was a mighty hunter. Hordes of dangerous animals roamed the land, and people lived in constant dread. Nimrod hunted and killed the animals, trying to make life safer for the people. He was regaled as a great hero and savior.

He even conceived of greater ways to defend the people by building walled cities, the first of which was Babylon. It's not hard to see why he was venerated, admired, and revered by the peoples of the world and why they looked upon him as the promised one.[2]

Nimrod organized Babylon into a great worldwide commercial center. Then he extended his influence into the surrounding areas, establishing his control and prominence.

He later developed a religious system that was based on the arrangement of the stars (known as the zodiac), from which comes the idea of astrology. The word babylon, which in Hebrew means "the gate of God," also comes from a similar Hebrew root word babel, which means "confusion."[3]

Mystery Babylon, Mother of Harlots, and Mystery Babylon, the Great City, are both mentioned in the book of Revelation as the end time promulgators of Satan's program for world control. If the physical Babylon had remained, today it would be located in present-day Iraq.[4]

**Nimrod, an Antichrist**

It can be seen that Nimrod, the humanitarian heralded as a savior of the world, was a classical antichrist type. He led the people away from worshiping the living God and into idolatry. Instead of God being the focus of worship, Nimrod became the focus of worship.

He taught the worship of life through mystery religions and worship of the stars. He taught the worship of creation—and left the Creator out of the picture.[5]

The power of Nimrod's control over the known world can still be felt today. For example, the tradition of the Christmas tree during the season of the celebration of Jesus' birth is actually a stolen idea from the celebration of the birth of Nimrod. The Roman Catholic church adopted the idea, which was a world-renowned pagan tradition, and applied it to the birth of the Lord Jesus Christ.[6]

From the beginning, Satan's executive power on Earth has been behind the world political, economic, and religious empires, beginning with ancient Babylon. It will end with the Global World Government, the Beast.

Nimrod's Babylon is the foundation for the meaning of Mystery Babylon, Mother of Harlots. Nimrod's Babylon is the mother.

## Chapter Eleven

# Tracks in the Sands of Time

The following Scripture expresses, in symbolism, the panorama of Gentile world rule—from the Egyptian empire until the final Global World Empire is formed.

> "And the angel said unto me, Wherefore didst thou marvel? I will tell thee the mystery of the woman, and of the beast that carrieth her, which hath the seven heads and ten horns. The beast that thou sawest was, and is not; and shall ascend out of the bottomless pit, and go into perdition: and they that dwell on the earth shall wonder, whose names were not written in the book of life from the foundation of the world, when they behold the beast that was, and is not, and yet is. And here is the mind which hath wisdom. The seven heads are seven mountains, on which the woman sitteth. And there are seven kings: five are fallen, and one is, and the other is not yet come; and when he cometh, he must continue

> a short space. And the beast that was, and is not, even he is the eighth, and is of the seven, and goeth into perdition. And the ten horns which thou sawest are ten kings, which have received no kingdom as yet; but receive power as kings one hour with the beast. These have one mind, and shall give their power and strength unto the beast" (Revelation 17:7-13)

**The Seven Heads**

This scripture pictures a relationship between Mystery Babylon, who is called the Great Harlot, and the infamous beast upon which she is seated. Her seated position suggests that she is in control and being carried by the Beast.

Although much biblical scholarship has been put forth concerning the heads of the Beast as being mountains or hills (i.e., the seven hills of Rome are the mountains upon which the Harlot sits, the Great Harlot being Rome), Scripture goes on to point out that the seven mountains are seven kings. The angel says they are seven regal mountains, meaning seven kings, or seven great ruling powers. Those powers were preceding world empires.

A mountain, or prominent elevation on the surface of the earth, is one of the common scriptural image or representation of a kingdom, regal dominion, empire, or established authority. So King David, speaking of the vicissitudes which he experienced as the king of Israel says,

> "O Lord, by Thy favor Thou didst make my mountain to stand strong" (Psalm 30:7)

The Lord, in His threat against the throne and power of

Babylon, said:

> "Behold, I am against thee, O destroying mountain, saith the Lord, which destroyed the whole earth: and I will stretch out mine hand upon thee, and roll thee down from the rocks, and will make thee a burnt mountain." ( Jeremiah 51:25)

> "And the stone that smote the image became a great mountain, and filled the whole earth." (Daniel 2:35)

The seven heads are best and most accurately explained as seven kings. The symbolism of the mountains or heads merely represents seven successive kingdoms. It can be argued that, although heads may be kings or kingdoms, they should not be looked at in successive order. The fact that five of the heads had already fallen, one was then in existence, and one was still future answers that objection.

Since the issue of succession of kings is proved in the above scriptures, the identity of Mystery Babylon, Mother of Harlots cannot be just papal Rome. The woman sits upon empires that had already fallen before Rome existed, and she continues to outlive the empires that come and go.

She rides upon empires, kings, powers of the world; she inspires, leads, and controls them. She is above them all so that they court her and are bewitched and governed by her.

They are governed not with the reins of empire, but with the lure of her fornication. Mystery Babylon is none other than Nimrod's Babylon that continues to hold sway all through time, outliving each successive empire even to this day.

Her doom is at the end of time, when she will receive her judgment. She, therefore, fills up the whole interval of time from the foundation of Babylon, the city of Nimrod, until the end of the age.

**The Ten Horns**

The last great empire of the Gentile rulers (the eighth head coming out of the slain seventh head) will consist of a ten member confederacy which is essentially Roman in flavor with a ruling Antichrist.

The ten members of the Beast are spoken of as horns. A horn in Scripture is interpreted as a king or a kingdom. Daniel said:

> "Then I would know the truth of the fourth beast, and of the ten horns that were in his head.... And the ten horns out of this kingdom are ten kings that shall arise." (Daniel 7:19, 20, 24)

These ten kings or kingdoms give their power and authority to the Antichrist/Beast for one hour, or a short time.

The seven heads represented in the vision are seven world Gentile powers, or imperial heads, that have existed down through history.

These seven heads will be the subject of our focus over the next several chapters. Remember that the goal of this process of investigation will be the revelation of the identities of both the first and second Beasts of Revelation chapter 13. It is imperative that we study both Beasts, for it is through the identification of the first Beast that the necessary clues emerge for the identification of the second Beast.

**Seven Heads**

Each head in the symbol represents an imperial empire.

These imperial heads, along with the ten horns, comprise the entire Beast system that was, and is not, and is about to come. It can be seen from the scripture that the Beast will not be just a "last days" phenomenon, but that it has been Satan's executive agent existing in some form or another for more than five thousand years.

The last phase of the Beast system will evolve, coming to a climax when ten kings or kingdoms will arise and give their allegiance to the system and a man (the Antichrist) who will operate the Global World Empire. This evolutionary process began with the foundation of Babylon, the Mother of Harlots, and has proceeded through each successive world empire to the present. In Revelation 13:1, we see the system emerging slowly out of the sea. It comes up arising over time from the multitudes.

The construction of the Beast system corresponds with the words of Christ when he spoke of the "times of the Gentiles".

> "And Jerusalem shall be trodden down of the Gentiles, until the times of the Gentiles be fulfilled." (Luke 21:24)

The "times of the Gentiles" simply means the period of a time where the empires of the world are controlled by the Gentiles.

Many believe the times of the Gentiles ended when the state of Israel was formed in 1948. Others believed it ended when Jerusalem was recaptured by the Jews in 1967. Neither is correct. But the end of the Beast system will come with its destruction, when Christ returns to establish His theocratic kingdom on the earth for one thousand years.

> "Thou sawest till that a stone was cut out without hands, which smote the image upon his feet that were of iron

> and clay, and brake them to pieces.... And the stone that smote the image became a great mountain, and filled the whole earth."(Daniel 2:34-35)

This scripture points to the coming Kingdom of God, which strikes the existing governing Beast powers and topples them. It is a kingdom cut out without hands, which signifies a kingdom that is not man-made. It will come at the end of the world, and it alone will destroy the kingdoms (the Beast) of the Gentiles (see Daniel 2:44,45).

**The Spiritual Template**

Cainism and Mystery Babylon are, and always have been, the principle guiding powers of each subsequent and succeeding imperial head from its rise to its fall. These guiding powers will come to their zenith in the Antichrist's Global World Order. Revelation 17:10-11 provides a historical template showing each imperial head from the time of its beginning until the present.

**The Beast—The System**

> "And there are seven kings: five are fallen, and one is, and the other is not yet come; and when he cometh, he must continue a short space. And the beast that was, and is not, even he is the eighth, and is of the seven." (Revelation 17:10,11)

John saw the Beast as a system which had evolved over the course of history. Daniel, however, saw forward to the last stage of the Beast system, with the Antichrist and the ten horns at the very end of the age. When John spoke of the eighth head, he was speaking of a revived world imperial system that had recovered from a head wound, or, as the Scripture put it, the wound of a great sword.

> "And I saw one of his heads as it were wounded to death; and his deadly wound was healed: and all the whole world wondered after the beast." (Rev 13:3)

Today, there are some who think that the apostle was talking about a man that had been healed from a wound to the head. They believe that this alleged human being would then turn into the Antichrist, a satanic resurrection as it were. But Scripture speaks of an imperial head being resurrected, not a human being.

**Unlocking the Mystery**

To get at the mystery of who and what the eighth head is, we must see who the seventh head was because it precedes the eighth head (the eighth head is of the seven). Getting to the root of this mystery takes some digging; therefore, we must reconstruct the whole system in its entirety.

> "And there are seven kings: five are fallen, and one is"...(Revelation 17:10)

We will begin here with the statement "one is." What does this mean? This was clearly the world empire that existed during the time Jesus walked the earth. It was also the time when the apostle John was writing the great book of Revelation. It was the Roman Empire.

Moving backward from the Roman Empire, signified by the head that "is," the sixth head, there had been five world empires that had already fallen. They had disappeared from history as the ruling power of their time. They, when they existed, were of the same dominating class as the Roman Empire. A brief look at history tells us with unmistakable certainty who those five empires were.

**The Five that Had Fallen**

In retreating sequence (going backward in time), the five fallen empires were:

1. Greece, 330-145 BC
2. Medo-Persia, 558-330 BC
3. Babylon, 625-538 BC (under Nebuchadnezzar)
4. Assyria, 800-606 BC
5. Egypt,1 2500-1000 B.

These are the five kings that had fallen. Rome was the sixth, the one in Revelation 17:10 that "is."

The task ahead is to identify the empire that is called the seventh, from which comes the eighth. First we will briefly walk through the five fallen kings looking for clues to the identity of the last two empires, the seventh and the eighth empires.

# Chapter Twelve

## Nimrod of the Ancient World

Critical to understanding the five fallen kings is how the ancient Babylonian kingdom of Nimrod relates to the empires that would follow from it. Babylon, the mysterious system, is represented in the book of Revelation as a scarlet woman, or a prostitute, and is titled Babylon the Great, the Mother of Harlots, and of the Abominations of the earth (Revelation 17:5). In Egypt, according to Hislop, the worship of the patron god and goddess, Osiris and Isis, can be directly traced to Nimrod, founder of the great city of Babylon, and his wife Semiramis.[1]

Nimrod was a man of renown upon the earth. He advanced his kingdom from Babylon into Egypt, Assyria, and other parts of the world. His greatness as a mighty hunter and the protection he afforded the masses by fortifying the cities with walls gave him great admiration by the peoples of the earth.

It was through fortification that the peoples enjoyed peace and safety from the ever-present threat of wild beasts. Nimrod became legendary amongst the peoples for his mighty exploits.[2]

Hislop records that in his hunting expeditions Nimrod employed the horse, along with leopards, to track down animals. His renown became universal, and Nimrod was deified by men and hailed as a god and savior.

The ancient Babylonian coins which picture a centaur (half horse and half man) is the actual depiction and memorializing of Nimrod.[3]

Yet for all the good he did for the people in saving and protecting them from destruction, Nimrod turned their hearts from God and onto himself.[4]

**Desecrated Trinity**

In ancient times, the recognition of a Trinity was universal in all the nations of the world; however, in the pagan world it was overlaid with idolatry. Nevertheless, the corruption of the idea of the Trinity proved how deep-seated the idea was in the breast of men. Pagan religion was replete with symbols that attested to this idea of a triune God.[5]

It was during the Babylonian era that an important change occurred in the pagan concept of the Trinity. The triune God was clearly articulated in the Christian era, but during Nimrod's time there consisted a blasphemous idea of the Father, Seed (or Son), and Holy Ghost.

It came to be thought of as the eternal Father Spirit of God incarnate in a human mother and a divine son. As a result of this alteration in the original idea of the triune God, the first person of the Trinity, the Father, was overlooked. Now, with the change, the Babylonians focused their worship on a goddess mother and a son.[6]

Since Nimrod had expanded the sphere of his influence and power into Egypt, these people also began to worship the mother and the son under the names of Isis and Osiris: Isis the mother, Osiris the son.[7]

As Nimrod's fame spread, the Babylonian godhead became a universal focus of worship. In India, the gods Isi and Iswara are the counterparts of the Egyptian Osiris and Isis, and they are worshiped even to this day. In Asia, the same holds true with Cybele and Deous as the facsimile of the Egyptian duo.

In pagan Rome, it was Jupiter-puer. In Greece, the godhead was Ceres, the great mother with the babe at her breast, or Irene, the goddess of peace with the boy Plutus in her arms. Even in remote places such as Tibet, China, and Japan, evidences were found of this same pagan worship of a misunderstood idea of the Trinity.[8]

Hislop makes tremendous application of this perversion of the Godhead and its effect on papal Rome, where Mary and Jesus had become the Christian counterparts of Egyptian Isis (the mother) and Osiris (the son).[9]

**The Wife of Nimrod**

The depth of this mystery is great, with many turns in the road. To be able to arrive at some clarity of thought concerning the issue, we must go to the origin and centerpiece of the mystery: Nimrod and his wife Semiramis.

As time passed, Semiramis, known as the wife of Nimrod, evolved into a lofty position as mother of Nimrod as well. In Egypt, Isis was the mother and wife of Osiris, but these were merely Egyptian names attributed to the great fortress builder Nimrod and his wife/mother Semiramis. In Egypt, Osiris bore the title "husband of the mother."[10]

One last point needs to be hammered home before we press on to the next fallen king. In the ancient book of the prophet

Daniel, we read of a god called Ala Mahozine, the god of fortification (Daniel 11:38).

While Antiochus Epiphanes IV, the Syrian king, may have been the one being referred to in this text, history seems to be cyclical and very well may have a two-fold fulfillment. Since the spirit of Antichrist seems to honor a god of fortification, it is important to identify what and who this god was.

> "But in his estate shall he honour the God of forces: and a god whom his fathers knew not shall he honour with gold, and silver, and with precious stones, and pleasant things." (Daniel 11:38)

Although nowhere in antiquity can a god of fortification be found, there is great evidence of a goddess of fortification. Her name is Cybele, and she is always seen with her crown turreted, like the fortifications of towers. The reason for the towers of her crown was due to the fact that she erected towers in the cities she ruled over.[11]

Babylon was the first city erected after the ancient world was destroyed by the great flood. Ovid, the great historian, tells us that it was Nimrod's wife Semiramis, the first queen of that city, who was believed to have surrounded the city with brick walls. Semiramis, the deified queen, was the derivation of the worship of the goddess of fortifications. Cybele, with her turreted crown, was also known as Rhea; Semiramis was known as Rhea, and at times as well. Cybele was actually another name for Semiramis.[12]

But Semiramis (Rhea) did not build the walls alone. It has been kept as a matter of record by the Bible (and also through the ancient historian, Megasthenes) that it was Nimrod who surrounded the Babylonian city with the wall. Yet, Semiramis gained the glory because, in the esteem of the ancient idolaters, she held a higher position than Nimrod after his death.

All the characteristics and successes belonging to her husband were attributed to her. She was, however, the counterpart of the deity (that is, Nimrod deified) presiding over the bulwarks or fortress. From this we can see that the god of fortresses is none other than Nimrod. His deified name in Babylon was Ninus (meaning, "the son").[13]

**Egypt, FreeMasonry and the New World Order**

It is an admitted fact that the secret system of Freemasonry was originally founded on the mystery religion of the Egyptian Isis, the goddess mother/wife of Osiris. In Isis—the Egyptian counterpart for Semiramis, Nimrod's deified wife/mother—we have a very important connection with Mystery Babylon of the Masonic lodges of the church era in the Western world, both in Europe and the United States of America.

What could have united the Masonic body and its mysteries—if the mysteries had not had particular reference to architecture and building and had the god of the mysteries not been celebrated for perfecting the arts of fortification and building?

These mysteries of Freemasonry, learned from Egyptian mythology and indirectly from Babylon, would be applied to fortress Earth—the obvious relationship of Freemasonry to empire building and global planning for a New Global World Order.

# Chapter Thirteen

# Five Kingdoms that Fell

**The First Fallen King: Egypt**

The Egyptian civilization arose after Nimrod's ancient Babylon, and it is believed to be more than forty-five hundred years old.

The Egyptian people were a very spiritual people and firmly believed in an afterlife. They held to the Babylonian notion of a pantheon of gods, and their spiritual history is well-documented.

The most important archeological discoveries of their religious history can be found in the Valley of the Kings in Luxor, Egypt. There, on the walls of the caves of the entombed pharaohs, are the hieroglyphic codes that have maintained the record.[1]

The character of the images kept on the walls of the caves suggests a very curious sense of how the Egyptians perceived the spiritual world. The deities pictured have animal heads and human bodies. Such a strange synthesis suggests an implied quality of the animal and made identification of the deity easy.

The temple of Karnak was the country's largest, and it was dedicated to the god Amun Ra, the sun god. The most important gods, however, were Osiris and his wife Isis. Osiris ruled over vegetation and the dead. Isis represented the devoted mother and wife. Their son was Horus, the god of the sky.[2]

When kings ruled ancient Egypt, the Egyptians believed that each of the pharaohs was Horus in human form. This legend greatly strengthened the authority of the kings. Strengthened by this myth, their authority had tremendous impact on every aspect of the people's daily life.[3]

Although the earliest beginning of Egyptian society dates back some five thousand years, it wasn't until 1554-1304 BC that Egypt became the world's strongest power. Much of the prominence and power of the nation was a result of a large and permanent army and their advanced military techniques, which they had learned from earlier periods. The Egyptians also developed a galley-powered navy with which they made many military conquests into Southeast Asia.[4]

This great world empire, the first of the five heads of the Beast mentioned in Revelation, reached its height around 1400 BC under King Thutmose III when he brought Palestine and Syria under Egyptian control.

The infamous Ramses II, the oppressor of the Hebrews, reigned during Egypt's five hundred years of world dominance known as Dynasty XIX. It was during his reign, however, that the great Egyptian empire began to decline.[5]

### The Second Fallen King: Assyria

Clearly, the influence of Nimrod was established in Assyria, as Scripture points out in the book of Genesis. The principal city of Assyria even bears the name of Nimrod (Ninus, his name deified, is the principal root of the city's name, Nineveh).[6]

The Assyrian king was known as the great king, the legitimate king, the king of the whole world. In the Assyrian kingdom the figure of a bull represented the king; the same word that signified bull also signified a ruler or a prince. The horned bull signified the mighty prince, which was a direct throwback to Nimrod, and represented all the great Assyrian kings.[7]

Although the Assyrian civilization can be traced back to 2000 BC, its empire building actually took place around 800-606 BC. The story of Assyria is mainly a story of the Assyrian kings. Some of the greater kings were Shalmaneser, Tiglath-pileser, and Esarhaddon. These kings, along with others, led a proud, cruel, and warlike race.

In many respects they were much like Rome. Just as Rome welded all the peoples of the Mediterranean world into a great empire, then scattered seeds of her civilization throughout the world, so did Assyria weld into a great empire the numerous petty warring states and tribes of Western Asia. Afterward, she spread her civilization throughout her extended domains, which to a great degree she had received from conquered Babylon.[8]

As the empires that succeeded her evolved and came to the forefront, it is not an exaggeration to say that the great civilization of Greece owes much of her architecture, sculpture, science, philosophy, and mathematical knowledge to the Assyrian Empire.

Assyria was a mighty power for hundreds of years, but after the mid-600s BC, she declined as a world empire. Babylon was again coming to the forefront as a world power.[9]

The mighty influence of Nimrod's Babylon (Mother of Harlots) can be clearly seen in the Assyrian Empire.

**The Third Fallen King: Babylon**

Babylon had two runs as a world empire: Nimrod's Babylon, which was recorded in Genesis chapter 10, and dates back to 3000 BC; and Babylon, which arose to supplant the Great Assyrian Empire during the 600s, reaching its peak from about 625-538 BC.[10]

The question might be asked, why was Nimrod's Babylon of old not considered as the first of the five fallen kings mentioned in Revelation 18?

A good, but improper, answer would be that if you started with Nimrod's Babylon, you then would proceed forward to Egypt, then Assyria, Babylon again, Medo-Persia, and Greece. This would equal six fallen kings and would be too many to fit into the prophecy.

It could then be argued, however, that beginning with Egypt and finishing with Greece is forcing the Scripture to say what one would want it to say. Nimrod's Babylon should be the beginning point!

This point of view is not an unfair argument, but when the whole of Revelation 17 is looked at, it becomes clear why this is not so.

> "And there came one of the seven angels which had the seven vials, and talked with me, saying unto me, Come hither; I will shew unto thee the judgment of the great whore that sitteth upon many waters: With whom the kings of the earth have been made drunk with the wine of her fornication. So he carried me away in the spirit into the wilderness: and I saw a woman sit upon a scarlet colored beast, full of names of blasphemy, having seven heads and ten horns. And the woman was

> arrayed in purple and scarlet color, and decked with gold and precious stones and pearls, having a golden cup in her hand full of abominations and filthiness of her fornication: And upon her forehead was a name written,
>
> "MYSTERY, BABYLON THE GREAT, THE MOTHER OF HARLOTS AND ABOMINATIONS OF THE EARTH."(Revelation 17:1-5)

From this Scripture it can be seen that Nimrod's Babylon is the fountainhead, or the progenitor, of all the world's empires and sits atop them as a ruling power. It is the ruling posture of the woman (Nimrod's Babylon) that elevates her importance above the succeeding fallen kings (beginning with Egypt and ending with Greece thus eliminating her as one of the fallen kings. As we continue on, each successive king emanates from her (Nimrod's Babylon) and continues to have intercourse with her. She is the mother of harlots.

Modern Babylon, or the second emergence of Babylon around 600 BC, in her magnificence, is still talked about, with her hanging gardens that many consider one of the great wonders of the world. The great walled city built by Nebuchadnezzar, who later attacked Judah and carried the Jews off, was considered impregnable. The city was so tightly secured that the people had absolutely no fear of ever being attacked or overtaken.[11]

**The Prophet Daniel in Babylon**

The prophet Daniel prophesied during the time of the Babylonian captivity of the Jews, when the Babylonians had carried them off to Babylon. God had given him a revelation of the world empires that would succeed from the time of the

Babylonian era all the way until the end of time.

During a dream he saw the world empires represented in a giant figure. The body parts of the statue represented each successive kingdom that would arise. The head of the figure, which was made of gold, represented Babylon; the shoulders and chest, made of silver, represented Medo-Persia; the hips, made of bronze, represented Greece; and the legs, made of iron, represented Rome. The feet were made of iron and clay, which relate to the last stages of the Roman Empire.

Daniel saw these world empires again in a later vision. In the later vision, the empires were depicted to him as animals or beasts. (Daniel 7:3-7)

**The Beasts**

Daniel saw Babylon as a lion, Medo-Persia as a bear, Greece as a leopard, and Rome—different from all the rest—as a beast that had ten horns. These ten horns corresponded to the ten toes of the feet in the first vision of world empires represented by the statue.

When the Jews were carried off to Babylon, strange things began to happen to their customs and traditions. Prior to their captivity, the Jews had been given the Law of God in the Ten Commandments and various other statutes at Mount Sinai. These regulations were God's plan for how Israel was to be governed. God's regulations covered every aspect of their life, including holidays, customs, and behaviors that were in accordance with the Mosaic law (as passed down in the book of Leviticus).

Whether it was the temple purification rites, the concept of the blood atonement wrought through animal sacrifices, the civic responsibility of the citizens, or even the cultural aspects of their society, the Law ruled over all and was the absolute guide of the people. The Law was absolute referee, whether for one's conscience or for the state.

The Hebrew nation was truly a peculiar nation, a chosen people different from all the rest. They were set apart from all the Gentile nations, who fashioned their civilizations out of Nimrod's Babylonian culture.

The Gentile's governing ideologies came from abstract notions about their deities, myths, and lore which originated from Nimrod's Babylon, the Mother of Harlots. In this remarkable way, the world's empires—each arising and succeeding the other until today—have committed acts of immorality and have become drunk with pagan tradition and worship. Even today the Washington monument, which is an Egyptian obelisk ( a phallic symbol of Nimrod), is a reminder of how extensive the effect of Mystery Babylon.

The Babylonians had their gods and goddesses, Bel or Bal, and Astarte and Ishtar, the goddess from whom comes the present Easter celebration. This is just a small indication as to how Babylon affects the world even today. But the evidence as to how Babylon has impacted the world throughout time is enormous.

**The Law of Moses Diluted**

It was during the Babylonian captivity of the Jews that much of the orthodoxy of the Mosaic law and its keeping began to be undermined and diluted by the culture of the pagan Babylonian Empire and its pervasive influence.

In Babylon, the Jews began to elevate the oral tradition above the written Law. Now, having been exiled to a far off land and without the centerpiece of their faith (the temple), the Jews had no purification rites available through animal sacrifices.

The blood sacrificial system was ripped away from them. As a result, the corporate conscience of Israel began to compromise the Law. Special addenda to the literal interpretation of the Law were added, compromising the truth in a vain attempt to absolve the national conscience.

The oral tradition evolved and then was formalized with the Talmud, which is the written version of the oral tradition. As the national conscience retreated and darkened, the selected people of God began to entertain Babylonian Mysticism and the occult.

**Babylon - the Root of Jewish Mysticism**

The influence of Babylonian mysticism on the Jews has endured through the centuries. Even to this present day, Jews consult and religiously study the Kabbalah, which is the Jewish book of the occult taken from their time of captivity in Babylon.

The derivation of the Kabbalah was the ancient Nimrodian system which had been handed down to Babylon during the time of Nebuchadnezzar. In Babylon (the third fallen king), the Jews learned to sin the sin of the pagan nations: spiritual fornication with the Mother of Harlots.

**The Fourth Fallen King: Medo-Persia**

In the later part of the sixth century BC, the ancient history of the Near and Middle East culminated in the establishment of the Persian Empire (558-330 BC) by Cyrus and Darius the Great.

In remote times, some Aryan tribes separated themselves from other members of their families and sought new places to dwell on the plateau of Iran. The tribes who settled to the south became known as the Persians, while those who settled in the northwest mountain region became known as the Medes. The names of the two peoples were always closely associated.[12]

The Persians were destined to become the dominant tribe. Eventually, the Persian kings ruled over Egypt, Palestine, Syria, Asia Minor, Mesopotamia, Iran, and, for a time, northwestern India and Trace. The empire stretched from the Mediterranean to Central Asia, and from the Black and Caspian Sea to the Persian Gulf and Indian Ocean.[13]

Under Cyrus the Great (whom Isaiah called "the servant of the Lord" some fifty years before Cyrus was even born; see Isaiah 45:1), the Medes and the Persians built a vast empire which lasted more than two hundred years.[14]

The empire—which was centered in Persia and called the Achaemenid Empire—included most of the known world. The Medes and the Persians came to power by the overthrow of the great Babylonian Empire. God had told Daniel that this was going to happen because the Babylonians had gone too far in oppressing the Jews (Isaiah 43:14).

The impregnable city of Babylon was captured by diverting the Euphrates River. The Medes and Persians then entered underneath the great walls through the conduits where the river had watered the city.[15]

The fall of Babylon automatically carried with it a claim to the Babylonian possessions in the west. In both Syria and Palestine, the native peoples welcomed Cyrus as a liberator. He reciprocated by respecting local traditions and religious practices. The Jews of the exile were permitted to return to Jerusalem and to rebuild the temple.[16]

**Persian Art Reveals Mystery Babylon**

The Persians and Medes took their ideas of art from the Egyptians and the Babylonians, and they, too, worshiped gods and goddesses of nature, such as the sun, sky, and fire. They even believed that their gods had social powers, and so their lives, like those of the great empires before them, were highly controlled by myths.[17]

When Persia invaded Greece in the early 400s BC, it was the beginning of the end. The Greeks were able to stop the expansion of that empire and to expel the invaders. Then came Alexander the Great, who in 331 BC conquered the Medo-Persian Empire. His empire lasted from 323-145 BC.

**The Fifth Fallen King: Greece**

During the time of Christ, Rome ruled the world, but Greece ruled the minds of men. Greece was the birthplace of Western Civilization.

Greece gave the world Plato and his most famous student, Aristotle. But, advanced as Greece had become in the study of law, medicine, philosophy, and public speaking, they, too, believed that a pantheon of deities watched over them.[18]

Dionysus, or Bacchus, the god worshiped in Greece, was expressly identified with Osiris of Egypt, who, as we have mentioned, may have been Nimrod (according to the great historian, Orpheus).[19]

Bacchus is often seen in pictures holding an ivy branch in one hand and a cup in the other. The devotees of Bacchus carried the ivy branch bound around their necks, carried in their hands, or indelibly stamped on their bodies. This was because the Greek word for ivy was kissos, and Kissos was one of the names of Bacchus. Further, it must be noted that the name of Cush (who was the father of Nimrod) was properly pronounced "Kissioi" in Greek.

It was through the name Cush that the priests became

familiar with the ancient mysteries. Since Kissioi means Cush, then the branch of ivy that was of such prominence in all the Bacchanalian ceremonies was an express symbol of Bacchus himself.[20]

Bacchus as the son of Cush, none other than Nimrod, took on the name of his father Kissos, the Greek for ivy. In fact, he was even called "The Real Branch." One of the names of the Messiah, as expressed in the book of Isaiah, was exactly that name: "The Branch."

Attributing the name of the son of God to a pagan deity is utmost blasphemy. So the cup in the hand of the Great Harlot of Revelation, which is full of blasphemous names, can be seen in the Greek worship of Bacchus, or old Nimrod. The relationship of the Greek religion to the ancient Babylonian Nimrod comes through clearly.[21]

Can the multitude of names attributed to Nimrod—in symbolic form and from empire to empire—be anything other than the names that fill the cup of the Harlot who sits on top of the seven-headed and ten-horned beast of Revelation?

> "So he carried me away in the spirit into the wilderness: and I saw a woman sit upon a scarlet coloured beast, full of names of blasphemy, having seven heads and ten horns. And the woman was arrayed in purple and scarlet colour, and decked with gold and precious stones and pearls, having a golden cup in her hand full of abominations and filthiness of her fornication." (Revelation 17:3,4)

Nimrod's Babylon is the Mother of Harlots that has deceived the whole world, even to this day. Examples can be found in the Christianizing of pagan holidays such as Easter (originally the worship of Astarte) and Christmas (Birth of Nimrod, son of Cush).

Very briefly, the first five world empires that are mentioned in Revelation 17 as having fallen—which correspond to the first five heads of the Beast—have been put forth.

Where they all came from has been explained, along with how they were shaped and influenced by their mother, Nimrod's Mystery Babylon, the Mother of Harlots.

To recap, here they are again (this time from oldest to youngest in their ascending order):

1. Egypt
2. Assyria
3. Babylon
4. Medo-Persia
5. Greece

And there are seven kings: five are fallen, and one is... Revelation 17:10

The sixth kingdom is Rome.

# Chapter Fourteen

## Rome: The Sixth Empire

The empire that began according to tradition by the twin brothers, Romulus and Remus, two shepherd boys, grew from a small community of sheep herders to an enormous empire of more than seventy million people. The city was situated next to the Tiber River atop seven hills (actually there are eleven hills), and far enough inland that it was protected from marauding bands of pirates. These natural barriers protected the city, and enabled Rome to grow over the centuries, becoming the sixth empire of the world.[1]

Its beginnings date back to 735 BC, and by 275 BC. It controlled most of the Italian peninsula. Rome peaked at about a.d. 100 and fell in ad 476. During its peak, it extended as far north as the British Isles, and as far east as Persia. Rome was the capital city of the Roman Empire, and it was inhabited by more than two million people at its height. The glue that held the empire together was the Pax Romana, the Roman peace.[2]

The peace was maintained by a huge army that continued

to grow as immigrants trickled into the empire, many of whom were recruited into the military. The army had three hundred thousand men.

The Roman law was the rule, enforced by the might and strength of the military which brought this peace.

Although republican institutions of government were kept throughout the history of the empire the emperors were the ones who held absolute rule. They nominated the consuls and appointed new senators. The citizens' assemblies had little power. Emperors also headed the army and directed the making of the law. The authority of the Roman emperor overruled any act of the Senate.[3]

After an emperor died, the Romans worshiped that emperor as a god, similar to the Egyptians' worship of the pharaoh. It was emperor worship that provided a common base of loyalty throughout the empire.

The Romans adopted the worship of the Greeks. They believed that the gods controlled nature, but they changed the names of the Greek gods to Roman names. The emperors were the supreme voice of the land superstitiously submitting to the pagan gods.[4]

Although much great romantic literature has been written about Rome, the prophet Daniel saw it as a ferocious beast. He spoke of Rome in more violent terms than all the rest of the world empires that had come before it (Daniel 7:7).

It was a restless kingdom that was not content with its size, and it continually overwhelmed new areas of land and peoples. Perhaps the reason for its fall in ad 476 was due to its own weight.

The Roman Empire must be remembered for the fact that it relished in the spectacle of organized murder in the gladiatorial games, where men actually died for the amusement and enjoyment of the emperor and the populace. It was also for great sport that Christians were fed to lions.

But foremost, Rome must be remembered for being the sixth great empire of the world, and murderer of the King of Kings. What an epitaph! It was the empire that the apostle John wrote of when he said, "five are fallen, and one is," ( Revelation 7:10)

## Chapter Fifteen

# The Seventh Head

> "And I stood upon the sand of the sea, and saw a beast rise up out of the sea, having seven heads and ten horns, and upon his horns ten crowns, and upon his heads the name of blasphemy."(Revelation 13:1)

Historical ignorance creates a kind of blindness that obstructs the ability to see things panoramically. If one cannot see where he has come from, he certainly will not see where he is going. When it comes to knowledge of world history, Americans, including Christians, have very little understanding or knowledge of the past.

But of greater significance and perplexity is the historical dearth of knowledge within the great theologians and spiritual leaders of the North American and European church. As a result, the parishioners inherit the ignorance.

In America, the willingness to be coaxed along in a red-blooded American nationalism seems to blind them to a truly objective understanding of who Americans are and where we came from.

**American Roots**

When it comes to an understanding of Great Britain, the mother country, Americans are almost totally in the dark. Americans have become ingrown and isolated from the world by their tremendous wealth and the great oceans that surround them like a moat. These factors have created a corporate aloofness that insulates this nation from the rest of the world. Most Americans simply do not care about historical facts relating to their own national identity, let alone any other country.

As the world stampedes toward a New Global World System, Americans must not lose sight of their European roots lest they become disoriented and miss an objective understanding of who they are as a people.

Since America was founded and established by Europeans, namely refugees from Great Britain, there should be at least a modicum of knowledge concerning the mother country.

The roots of the American spirit began with the corporate soul of the founding forefathers, who came from Great Britain. Hence, we should study the environment that shaped those men who laid the foundation for this great and powerful nation.

**Great Britain**

The history of Great Britain tells how a small island off the mainland of Europe grew to become the world's most powerful empire. During the time of its existence, and in the context of all history, there had not been a world empire like the British Empire. It even surpassed Rome in its might.

It was the industrial revolution of the 1700s that made

Britain the world's richest manufacturing country. After 1815, the city of London became the Vatican of world banking.2 The Empire was so enormous that the sun never set on it. By 1799, the empire covered about a fourth of the world's land and about a fourth of its people.[3]

Since people generally do not like to speak in disparaging terms concerning their own heritage, it is a difficult chore to lay bare the truth of the British Empire without bringing some degree of offense. Nonetheless, there are vital hidden facts about the British Empire, which make biblical prophecy ever more clear.

Consider the thoughts conjured in the mind of English-speaking people when they speak of the British Empire. What was the British Empire? What really was behind this allegedly called Christian empire?

In searching world history from the time of the fall of the Roman Empire, no other world empire had arisen since then, except the British Empire. It is the only one.

Is it possible that the British Empire is represented by the seventh head of the Beast of Revelation chapter 13?

**The Apostle John's Vision**

The apostle John saw a vision while exiled on the Isle of Patmos in AD 90. In symbolic form, he saw a beast coming up out of the sea. It had seven heads and ten horns. Six of these heads have already been identified in the preceding chapters, and now, as history is searched since the fall of the sixth head Rome, another world empire, the British Empire, has arisen.

> "And there are seven kings; five are fallen, and one is, and the other is not yet come."( Revelation 17:10)

But for some strange reason, neither North American

nor Northern European theologians have ever considered the emergence and existence of the British Empire as the fulfillment of the seventh head of the Beast.

The fact is, the British Empire is the only world empire that qualifies since the fall of the Roman Empire, and therefore, the only possible fulfillment.

The amazing power of this vast, worldwide empire did not reach its zenith—and its true status as undisputed ruler of the earth—until Napoleon was defeated at the Battle of Waterloo in 1815. When the British finally conquered the French, the British Empire ruled the world for about one hundred years, from 1815 until the outbreak of World War I.[4]

**The Global Rule**

In 1815, the British Empire, the seventh imperial head of John's Beast, emerged as supreme power over the area that essentially encompassed the old Roman Empire. The Global Rule

However, while the British Empire increased in power, it was specifically accruing to the revenues of The City under the crown, not to England itself. The city of London fell under the control of an elite group of bankers, the Rothschilds (more explanation of this international elite will be given shortly).[5]

The City today controls over eighty percent of all international business transactions. England itself was bled dry by this hidden inner government and was harnessed for the special aims of The City, which became the seat for an International Global World Government.[6]

The internationalists (the bankers) have no feeling of nationalism or patriotism towards any nation, including England. England—once Christian-controlled, to a degree, under the influence of the Protestant Reformation—fell under the power of "mammon," or money, controlled by the international money cabal (the Rothschilds).[7]

(Note—this is not to dismiss the important workings of the Holy Spirit in England during those times. God did profound things in the eighteenth and nineteenth centuries in England. The religious zealots who founded the United States were people who came from Britain and had a deep, orthodox knowledge of the Scriptures. But the secular English state tried to control the operation of the true church, and this became intolerable for true believers. This was one of the key motivating issues for their exodus to the New World.)

**The East India Company**

Little, if any, is known in the Western Hemisphere of the nefarious ways in which the British Empire gained its supremacy over the Earth. However, the peoples of India and China can give grim testimony to the most notorious of all the terrible war machines of conquest that the Empire possessed: the infamous East India Company.[8]

The company was formed in 1600 when, following the defeat of the Spanish Armada, Queen Elizabeth granted a charter to certain London-based merchants to trade in the East. The company grew stronger as it became ensconced in worldwide trade. It was allowed to have monopolistic privileges in return for a fraction of its earnings, and so it gained tremendous financial might. As it grew, it built a large private army which contested with the French and Dutch traders and learned methods of control and looting in India.India became controlled by bribery and graft as the company set up a puppet government, which then imposed forced sales of merchandise and outright looting through tax collecting.

If the people resisted, various methods of compulsion were practiced—such as fines, imprisonment, and floggings—forcing the people to submit.[9]

The British taxed the people to exhaustion, and when famine conditions arose in 1770 due to poor weather, ten million people in Bengal starved to death.[10]

**The East India House**

Towards the end of the seventeenth century, when America's war for independence from the iron-like grip of British dominion was succeeding, the political circles associated with the British East India Company seized nearly complete control over British political party affairs. The historical significance of this event—and its subsequent effect on world affairs—has been monumental, and yet it is completely neglected in this hemisphere.[11]

A new prime minister came on the scene: William Petty. At that time Petty negotiated the peace treaty with the America. (after the war for independence). He also directed British intelligence services in a complex worldwide task of conquest and subversion. Even though the American Revolution had succeeded, in the eyes of this man it was not the end of the effort to subjugate the American colonies to British control.[12]

Over in India, a board of control for the affairs of India was set up under the leadership of Henry Dundas. Dundas controlled the Indian operation for thirty years, during which time he proposed that Indian opium be poured into China as an instrument of war and looting. Dundas was also the man to whom Aaron Burr, vice president to Jefferson, reported in England.

In 1787, Dundas wrote a master plan to extend the opium traffic into China, and he personally supervised the worldwide traffic of opium which had been escalated by the East India Company.[13]

After the war, General Cornwallis, the British general who surrendered at Yorktown, was reassigned by Dundas to be commander in chief and governor general over India. Britain was gearing up for a military offensive over all Asia. Finally, in 1803, the British East India Company subdued and controlled the entire subcontinent of Asia. The army had now swelled to more than a quarter million men, and the navy patrolled the seas from the southwest Pacific to the Persian Gulf. This power engaged in conflict after conflict, inflicting fatalities in the millions,[14] but people in the Western Hemisphere are routinely ignorant of such facts of history.

To further loot India, the British raised high tariffs but kept India open for British goods. India paid for its imported goods from Britain with opium from plantations developed by the British. The opium was sold to the Chinese to oppress them and to raise money to pay for the British goods sold to India.15

The peasantry, those who cultivated cotton, were treated with savage and revolting actions. They were subjected to torture and every effort—lawful or unlawful—to extract revenues. When they tried to run away from this brutal treatment, they were rounded up by the British, flogged, and put back to work. As the nation's cotton began to disappear due to this kind of treatment, the exploiters looked to American slave cotton as a viable alternative source of cheap raw material.[16]

The British occupation of India was maintained and manipulated by a cunningly devised cultural warfare. The idea for maintaining control was to prevent any and all importation of Western ideals or values into western India.[17] The East India Company patronized and advanced the most outrageous aspects of the pagan Indian religions and made Hinduism and Islam British state-run religions.

When the British finally turned their gaze upon America, the technique they used was to displace the Western Christian beliefs of the American people by importing and introducing Eastern Indian religious beliefs, thus undermining Western values. The drug wars can also be traced to the East India House strategy.[18]

## Chapter Sixteen

# The 7th Head..... continued

"To destroy a country," Alexandr Solzhenitsyn wrote, "you must first cut its roots." If America's roots are in the Judeo-Christian values and traditions, they have, in large measure, been severed. Today, of course, the root base of the philosophy of the New Age movement is directly taken from Indian Hinduism. Notwithstanding, one does not have to look to far to see the monstrous effect of Islam on the Judeo- Christian ethic.

**John Stuart Mill**

The chief intelligence officer of the East India Company into the 1900s was John Stuart Mill, who ran the evil organization from London. When the Indians revolted in 1857, the atrocities of that conflagration so outraged the world that Queen Victoria stepped in, and within a few years the East India Company was dissolved. But the industrious John Stuart Mill turned his attention to the fledgling nation of America. He was ready to apply the knowledge gained from his many years of experience in India to the conquest of America.[19]

Before we delve into the subversion of America by the East India Company, it must also be said that the East India House in London became the central point of interaction and dialogue for the main antagonists of Western Civilization. This central location became the seat of the existential writers that focused on a theology of man as the center of all things.

The propagators of this "anglicized Hinduism" were men like Henry David Thoreau and Ralph Waldo Emerson. Charles Darwin was also, contemporary with these men, and he associated with them at the East India House. Their doctrine was the philosophical base from which worldwide cultural warfare would be launched.[20]

The advancement of the New Age Globalism movement can actually be traced directly to this think tank which operated in London at the East India House run by John Stuart Mill, the oppressor of India.[21] These men did not believe in the creed of all men being created equal but, quite the contrary, that all men by nature were created unequal: that some were meant to rule and others to be ruled over.

They saw the biblical definition of man submitting to a sovereign Lord God as repugnant to their dreams of globalism. Empire building, in their thinking, began with a definition of man as central, and from that point all considerations would proceed. The colonies in America, which were becoming more and more prosperous under the biblical theology and definition of man, had to be finally conquered and brought under control.[22]

**Government and Man's Nature**

The American Constitution was built upon a foundation

that had its roots in a biblical definition of man. The writers viewed man as having fallen from a divine position with God. They saw that man had become corrupted and that he has a sin nature. The founding fathers reasoned that because absolute justice and objectivity was possessed by God alone, no man, by himself alone, was fit to rule. They wrote the Constitution very cautiously. They placed checks and balances into the structure of the government so that one single man could never gain absolute control. They despised the monarchical system of Europe and England.

There were to be three branches of the federal government: executive, judicial, and legislative. Each branch was to ensure that one man nor group of men could gain absolute political power. It was deemed that each branch of government would balance the others. Tantamount in their thinking was the elimination and cruelty of despotism. This was the very issue over which they left England.

The framers of the Constitution had a keen sense of British history when they sat down to write the Constitution. They were flawed men for sure, but they clearly had in mind the historical facts of the tyranny of monarchical system in England.

### The Monarchical System

When Henry VIII became King of England in the sixteenth century, he was already wed to Catherine of Aragon. When he sought to divorce her and marry Anne Boleyn, it caused a separation between Henry and the Pope. The Roman Catholic Church refused to sanction the marriage. Nevertheless, King Henry went on with the marriage and was excommunicated from the Roman Catholic Church. Henry then ordered the English Parliament to declare the King as the supreme head of the Roman Catholic Church of England.

The separation of the Church of England from Rome effectively brought the Protestant Reformation to England. In 1534, by Henry's insistence, Parliament passed two acts that made the break complete. The first declared that the Pope had no authority in England. The second declared the Church of England a separate institution with the king as its head (the famous Supremacy Act). Both church and state had come under the authority of the king.

It was this act by King Henry VIII—bringing the religious and secular under one roof—that eventually led to the reasoning behind the first amendment of the United States Constitution. The spirit and intent of that amendment was not to eliminate religion from its influence on government but, quite the contrary, to keep government out of religion.

Later, both Henry's son and Queen Elizabeth caused the work of establishing the Church of England to go forward. Upon the arrival of the 1600s, England was ready to embark on a great era of development.

When the English, through the leadership of Sir Francis Drake, defeated the Spanish Armada in 1588, England had become the undisputed ruler of the seas. She now controlled all the shipping lanes, exacting tribute for maritime activities from all of Europe.

The last piece of contrivance for the realization of a Global World Empire was the ability to subjugate nations of the world through the sheer power of capital and credit.

**The Battle of Waterloo**

The opportunity for the seizure of "mammon" arose during Napoleon's attempt to seize Europe at the famous Battle of

Waterloo. How was the Battle of Waterloo utilized to further the aims of those who sought for a New World Order?[23]

First it must be understood that the real force of the French Revolution was not a spontaneous explosion within the corporate breast of the collective lower class of France. Historians have long blamed the masses for the revolution. However, enough facts have come to light to prove that France was infiltrated by subversives of the internationalists to destabilize her into a chaotic mass. Why was France selected as the beginning of the global revolution for a New World Order?[24]

The internationalists based in England saw in France a formidable opponent to the aims of the centralization of European capital.[25] France had to be destabilized into chaos. Then, with the important defeat of Napoleon, the opportunity arose to seize financial power into the hands of the money conspiracists. While the philosophical intrigue and planning to upset the unifying aspects of monarchical family intermarriage shifted temporarily to center on Bavaria and the German states[26], the war chest for world revolution was being concentrated and built in London.[27]

## The Rothschilds Seize Control

Here is how it occurred. Upon the Battle of Waterloo hung the future of the European continent. If Napoleon were successful, France would be the undisputed master of Europe. If Napoleon were defeated, England would reign supreme.[28]

Obviously, the success of Lord Wellington would have tremendous positive implications on the British stock exchange. With Nathan Rothschild positioned in London, the headquarters of the Rothschild banking dynasty, the stage was set for the soon-to-be financial rulers of the nations. As the armies closed in for the battle, the secret agents of the Rothschilds gathered the information to whisk back to London.[29]

When the outcome of the battle was known to Nathan Rothschild, he gave the signal for his people to begin quietly selling consuls (like bonds) on the stock market. As the consuls began to pour onto the market, it created a stampede that caused the market to fall and then cascade into a panic sell off. It was feared that Napoleon had won the battle and Rothschild was privy to this information.[30]

Unbeknownst to those outside his circle, Rothschild was manipulating the market downward so that he could buy up the consuls at five cents on the dollar. When the news hit that

The British had actually defeated Napoleon, the market

soared like an eagle. Thus, Rothschild and his banking kingdom had seized, in one day, the vast war chest for economic control of the nations.[31]

The Rothschilds were of Jewish descent, and England, being a Christian nation, was not inclined to allow Jews into positions of political decision-making. Rothschild's response to this racist policy was this: "I care not for the laws of the nations. Give me the wealth of the nations and I'll make the laws."[32]

**The Bank of England**

Now, with an understanding of the Rothschilds, we must backtrack through English history to the year 1694. This was the year the Bank of England, a privately owned bank called the Central Bank, was established. The establishing of the Bank of England was of no small importance in world history. It was utilized to advance the power of the City of London, hence, the entire affairs of the rapidly growing British Empire.[33]

When Rothschild pulled off his seizure of the British economic system, he also gained control of the Bank of England

and the City of London. With the demise of France and the English victory over Napoleon at Waterloo, England emerged in 1815 as the undisputed ruling power of Europe.

The power of "mammon" was now in their grasp, the monarchical headship was removed, the influence of the Church of England was minimized in state affairs, and all state matters were subjugated to the Barons of Finance.

## Chapter Seventeen

# The Humanitarian Mandate

> "And I saw one of his heads as it were wounded to death; and his deadly wound was healed: and all the whole world wondered after the beast."(Revelation 13:3)

Profound events in Europe were taking place that were setting the stage for the death of the empire by a blow of war.

Behind the internationalists' drive towards a Global One World Government is a strange, innate sense of humanitarianism. It's as though the mandate to convert the world to a global village is their providential lot. It is the same driving force that Cain had when he offered to God a sacrifice of vegetables: man's human effort to right his twisted conscience. Globalism is the epitome of man's effort to bring about peace.

The globalists seek to do this through the unification of the earth, but their misguided zeal is channeled through human contrivance and manipulation. The overriding mental gymnastics to bring this about is through the dialectic, the ends justify the means, or whatever it takes to get the job done. If it means trashing a human here or a nation there—whatever the cost—it is justifiable in light of the highly prized and desired goal. This is the rationale of those seeking global revolution and a New Global World Order.

**The Internationalists' Apparatus**

These internationalists seek the humanitarian goal of world "peace and safety." Their goal seems noble and virtuous, and, because of this, there are few who challenge their means. The means for pulling off this humanitarian extravaganza is quite a story. Ironically, the internationalists use the device of war as a means to peace.

The internationalists will always profit from war because it doubly indentures a nation. First, it causes a nation to borrow in order to build its war machine; second, the nation has to borrow again after the war to rebuild its infrastructure.

Initially, the creation of nuclear weapons also served the interest of the money powers. Indebted nations that would dare to think of repudiation or a debt moratorium were brought back into tow by the threat of nuclear attack. Nuclear weapons were the ultimate collection agency tool. But this nuclear exclusivity is no longer the private province of the internationalists. The world is far more volatile now than in the 50's and 60's.

# Chapter Eighteen

## World Wars I and II

When America's industrial might was harnessed by the creation of the Federal Reserve System, the mobilization of credit became available to finance a New Global World Order. All that needed to be done was to create a world war. Most historians will admit that although there were two world wars, World War I and World War II, were ostensibly one war with a period of cessation in between. They would also admit that the beginning of World War I had no apparent rationale behind it.

The Archduke of Austria was assassinated and, as a result, the whole world went to war. Why? To this day there seems to be no clear answer, unless one sees that the international bankers had everything to gain by a world war. After all, there would be great profit in making huge loans to so many countries.

The international debt that accumulated after these two wars staggers the imagination. What an incredible money machine! Remember:

"The borrower is servant to the lender." (Proverbs 22:7)

The gigantic cash flow from the interest of mega-loans to the nations would be used to create a New World Order after the pattern suggested by Engels and Karl Marx, whose principles were based upon Adam Weishaupt's Order of the Illuminati.[1]

**Woodrow Wilson**

During his second campaign to become president, Woodrow Wilson campaigned under the slogan, "He'll keep us out of the war." However, within only months of his inauguration he drew America into World War I. America began to borrow heavily, both to build up its war machine and to finance a war on the other side of the earth. Many claim that Wilson was a pawn in the game of international power and world politics.[2]

The "war to end all wars," as it was called, served the internationalists in two ways: it brought the world into terrific debt, and it prepared the nations to seek peace at any price. As the war dragged on, the nations became weary and were suffering from great debt. They were now prepared and ready to make sacrifices on the altar of peace and, to a great degree, their national sovereignty.

**The League of Nations**

A League of Nations was proposed by Woodrow Wilson, which was the first step toward organizing the world into a One World Global Government. Wilson, who was manipulated by his mentor, Englishman Colonel Edward House, put forth the plan for the League of Nations in his famous Fourteen Points.[3]

Wilson's plan for a New World Order was well received by all nations except one, the United States. Patriotic Americans saw the danger of such a setup and throttled the idea of the

League. Wilson failed, and he died a broken man. So did the bankers' first attempt for a New World Order.

**Council on Foreign Relations**

The Council on Foreign Relations (CFR) was created by the globalists after World War I because of the League's failure. Its purpose was to monitor and determine American foreign policy so that America's decision making with regards to the nations of the world was in step with their ultimate goal of a World Government. The groundwork for the CFR was laid by Colonel Edward Mandell House, who was acting as the internationalist agent in America.[4] More will be said in a later chapter on the CFR.

**The Russian Revolution**

During the final years of World War I, the Russian Revolution was carefully planned and tried. The Bolsheviks, trained in New York, were financed by the international Kuhn, Loeb & Company (a New York banking house) and were sent through Germany into Russia to overthrow the Czar.[5]

The Bolsheviks were aided by Max Warburg, who was brother to Paul Warburg, the architect of the Federal Reserve System. Max was in control of the German banking system.[6]

But why bring about the perfect neo-feudal state in Russia first?

The plotters had several reasons: It was the largest land mass between Europe and Asia, and the outbreak of globalism as a system could be more easily managed; its population was large enough to mobilize and easily conquerable; its technology was lagging and its financial power was easily assailable.

The setup for globalism in its final form would begin in Russia, but its conception and financing were formulated by the banking elite of Europe.[7]

As the bankers from Wall Street (J.P. Morgan & Co.) moved to rearm Germany, the aspiring Adolf Hitler viewed both the Bolshevik Revolution and the attempt for World Government through the League of Nations as a Jewish plot to take over the world. He saw the bankers as the principal movers and shakers in this gigantic effort.[8]

"The Protocols of the Learned Elders of Zion," of dubious origin, was cunningly leaked to Hitler by the world planners to deceive him, making him think the New World Order was a Jewish plot.[9]

**Seventh Head Slain**

World War II—which actually was a resumption of World War I—was, in the mind of the world planners, a necessary evil. The British Empire had to be dissolved.

The "great sword" that wounded the seventh head of the Beast was the one war (what we refer to as World Wars I and II) that brought the seventh head, the British Empire, to an end. After World War II, the British Empire ceased, but it should be carefully noted that the seat of global financial power remained in London, unscathed by war. In fact, the money powers became more powerful due to the massive indebtedness the wars created.

In the Bible it is asked, "Who is able to make war with [the Beast]?" (Revelation 13:4). Yet the seventh empire was killed by the sword of war. What entity, what government, what other opponent out there could launch a conflict against the seventh head?

When it can be seen how World War I and World War II were orchestrated by the international bankers—who had no allegiance to England or the British Empire, but merely used them for their purposes in accomplishing a Global World Empire—the question is answered. The seventh head was slain by a sword created by the City of London who were the international bankers..[10]

# Chapter Nineteen

## The Great Sword

Hitler's Third Reich was supported and built by international capital, much of it coming from Wall Street, as the internationalists prepared the world for another blood bath and another round of debt.[1]

The need for the resumption of conflict was evident in that without the United States in the League of Nations, a World Government was impossible. What was needed was more debt and more cries for peace. Hence, the war needed to be rekindled.

When Hitler arose and began to foment such vehement hatred toward the Jews, it was because he believed he saw a Jewish conspiracy in a group of Jewish bankers who had seized control of the world banking system. He failed to see that the small group of bankers also included Gentile banking houses.[2] Germany's woes were not the fault of world Jewry.

Hitler blamed the whole of Jewry for the heavy-handed shackles of the Treaty of Versailles which ended WWI. He believed Germany was in ruins due to the Jews.

Then, adding fuel to the fire, Hitler's hatred was enflamed by the falsified document of "The Protocols of the Learned Elders of Zion."[3] This document was allegedly smuggled into Germany and was widespread among the German people. The document was intended to be construed falsely by the Germans as a Jewish blueprint for a New World Order.

The document, in form, is almost identical to the eighteenth century "Protocols of the Illuminati." That there is some ongoing conspiracy seems historically factual. That there is a modicum of Jews involved is unquestionable. That it is confined to only a Jewish conspiracy is highly improbable.

Hitler incriminated and indicted a whole race of people because of a few Jews (the Rothschilds) who had joined a number of Gentile bankers and plunged the world into a sea of red ink. Hitler's fire of hatred and suspicion was reinforced when the Rothschilds proposed and backed the Zionist movement in Israel.

But there were multitudes of Jews living throughout Europe that were vehemently against a Jewish state. They were anti-Zionists and opposed to any state for the Jews. They argued that until the Messiah came there should not be a place for the Jews— until their king had come, there should be no kingdom.

The secrecy that has enshrouded the International Banking Cabal has allowed it to remain virtually unknown to the world as well as to world Jewry. Nonetheless, this banking elite seems to have a strong feeling toward Israel in that it was the Rothschilds who helped fund the re-establishment of the state of Israel. They were also behind the scenes in setting the stage for the Balfour Declaration.[4]

## Hitler's Reaction to the Jews

Some have claimed that Karl Marx was a Jew. It is true that Marx's family was of Jewish descent, but his parents converted to Protestantism before Karl's birth.[5]

Those who falsely claim that Marx was a Jew do so attempting to add credence to the claim for the Jewish conspiracy theory. Karl Marx was baptized Protestant. Later in his life, Marx turned from God and developed hatred toward religion in any form. Marx was atheistic, denying the God of Judaism as well as the God of Christianity.

It was Karl Marx who instigated the philosophy of communism that was so destructive towards Germany's nation building in the 1850s and 1860s. It is also true, however, in all fairness that in the Russian Revolution there were apostate Jews who hated religion, but had a politico-Zionism at heart.

It is true that at the helm of the finances for this global world rule were the Rothschilds (formerly the Bauers), who were of Jewish heritage background. This is what Hitler saw.[6]

Hitler's diabolical hatred toward the Jews stemmed from his perceptions that the Jews, as a people, sought to take over the whole world, and that the Rothschild-financed Bolshevik Revolution was another step toward that end. In many of his speeches he expressed this belief.

**The following is from a German newspaper:**

On February 24, 1920, an ex-corporal in the German army named Adolf Hitler and a group of professional anti-Semitic agitators, including Julius Streicher, Alfred Rosenberg, and Gottfried Feder, met in a Munich beer hall and founded a new National Socialist Party.

The core of their National Socialist (Nazi) Party program

was the racist doctrine that only those with German blood in their veins might be considered a citizen of Germany. Therefore, no Jew could belong to the German nation. The Nazis declared that anti-Semitism was the emotional foundation of their movement; every member of the Nazi Party was an anti-Semite.

Hitler, the Fuhrer (dictatorial leader) of the Nazi Party, proudly announced his anti-Semitism as well as his inhumanity.

> "Yes we are barbarians; we want to be barbarians; it is an honorable title. We shall rejuvenate the world; this world is near its end. We are now near the end of the Age of Reason. The Ten Commandments have lost their validity. Conscience is a Jewish invention. It is a blemish, like circumcision. There is no such thing as truth, either in the moral or in the scientific sense. We must distrust the intelligence and the conscience and must place our trust in our instincts. And was not the whole doctrine of Christianity, with its faith in redemption, its moral code, its conscience, its conception of original sin, the outcome of Judaism?"[7]

This last statement of Hitler's is the most revealing about the global conspiracy as he felt it related to the Jews.

"The struggle for world domination will be fought between us, between Germans and Jews." (Hitler)[8]

**Adolf Hitler**

Hitler's own attempt at world dominion was essentially an attempt to break out of the grasp of the international banking elite. But it did not help when much of the anti-semitism that pervaded the German populace actually hung like a cloud over the German population for centuries before Hitler. When Hitler arrived on the scene, Germans were already primed for his rant.

**The Reformation and the Holocaust**

The time has come to study the anatomy of the German political discord. Make no mistake about it, there is a clear spiritual connection between the Protestant Reformation and the Holocaust.

First of all, let me be clear, I am from Jewish genetics. I am not anti-semitic, and God has a special place in His heart for the Jewish people. He has indicated as much in the Bible, where it is very clearly stated they are beloved by God for the sake of the fathers. Unfortunately though, it also says they will become enemies of Yeshua ie. Jesus, and His followers.

Today, the force of their acrimony towards Christians has reached fever pitch as it did in the days of Hitler. The greatest megaphone mouthpiece for their dissidence is the liberal media, and that is because the liberal media is controlled almost exclusively by the Jews. But their anger is not without reason nor should it be altogether cloaked from understanding.

Why the mystifying attack and slander which came upon the president of the United States Donald Trump? After all, he was a resurgent champion of the Jewish state of Israel. The prime minister of Israel had even said as much. How could the Jewish liberal controlled media not have been aligned with the president when he strongly favored the Jewish state? It is almost as though the liberal Jews were aligning themselves with Islam which favored the total destruction of the Jewish state.

What's up with the conundrum and disconnect? How has this come to a climax in our present time? It is not as though anti-semitism should be relegated and viewed merely to the time of Christ. Even before the modern era post-Jesus times, anti-semitism can be traced as far back as 700 BC.

It was called by the Jewish prophet Jeremiah as "the ancient hatred." In fact anti-semitism can be noted even back to the time of Abraham, which was about 2000 BC. Abraham, while not a Jew, was a Hebrew; he was a descendant from the tribe of Eber (Hebrews). That evil spirit has been in the world since the time of the worship of the moon god of the Kabah. Hatred of the Jews has existed throughout time. Why? It is because it is an evil spirit that hates the fact that it was the Jews, and the lineage of Abraham, who gave the world the redeemer, even Jesus.

Today the liberal media Jews have not figured out that they have succumbed to the virulent and highly contagious disease of hatred.

One can see this evil force warring against these ancient people during the first century when the Romans destroyed their temple and city. It was the Roman, Hadrian, who changed the name of Jerusalem to Aelia Capitolina and their country of Israel to Palestine.

Several hundred years later the so-called Christian, Constantine, almost completely expunged them from the city of Jerusalem, and forced the few remaining Jews to the northern part of their country. There were virtually no Jews in the land for one thousand years. Later, Jews were forced to convert or be murdered by the Catholic Church in the time of the Spanish Inquisition.

It is generally unknown that Columbus, who was a Jew, was seeking in the new world a safe haven where the Jews could flee from the pogroms. He founded a place in Jamaica. It became a sanctuary for Jews to be free from Catholic oppression, and it remained for one hundred years.

Then came the reaction of the Reformation. Martin Luther,

the spearhead against the Catholic Church and who led the way for the Protestant Reformation, initially was compassionate towards the Jews. But He made a horrific mistake. It was when he excised and cut out the book of Revelation from canon of scripture. There are dire warnings in the book itself from adding to or taking away from the Revelation. Were anyone bold and reckless enough to do such a thing, it would bring down serious consequences.

Anyone or any nation which would take away from the book of Revelation would be in serious spiritual trouble. Consequently for the German people, their heart was hardened and turned on the Jews. The whole of the nation followed Luther and turned on the Jews. It is a matter of record they actually hated them. This brought about a surge of anti-semitism in Germany, that became an acidic cloud that hung over them for hundreds of years.

**Night of the Broken Glass**

Fast forward to the twentieth century and November 9, 1938. It was Luther's birthday. And not coincidentally it would become the night of the "broken glass." It was the very night of Kristallnacht.

Hitler purposely and selectively chose that night to celebrate and launch the Holocaust in commemoration of Luther. It was as though he was using Luther as the figurehead to underwrite his hatred of Jews. In using Luther Hitler by association implicated the Church.

This was no coincidence. Kristallnacht was the starting point for the Holocaust. Luther's hatred of the Jews actually was praised by Adolph Hitler. Luther, it can be said, actually paved the way for the third Reich.

Since the Protestant churches were launched by the

Reformation instigated by Martin Luther, Christianity in general as viewed by the Jews, has been associated with Nazism. The Jews have a long memory of these matters, and now that they have by and large gained control of the media, they use it to express their own brand of hatred.

In fact, anything the Christians put their hand to is viewed by Jews as a product of Nazism.

The very man God selected, a man hailed as one of the greatest theologians and Christians of all time, stumbled over his own brilliance. Had he taken heed to Revelation 12, we may have had a different world.

# Chapter Twenty

## The Satanic Resurrection

> "And I saw one of his heads as it were wounded to death; and his deadly wound was healed: and all the whole world wondered after the beast." (Rev. 13:3)
>
> Here in Revelation 13 is a resurrection of the seventh head which had been slain. The resurrection is actually mentioned three times. In Revelation 17, the resurrection is also mentioned.
>
> "And the beast that was, and is not, even he is the eighth, and is of the seven." (Revelation 17:11)

These scriptures must all be looked at together. How can chapter thirteen shows seven heads where the seventh is slain by a great sword and comes back to life, while in chapter seventeen the resurrection of the seventh head is spoken of as an eighth head, which comes out of the seven? Why didn't the Holy Spirit, who inspires all Scripture, say something like this:

"I looked and saw the seventh head resurrected," and leave it at that? Why does he say in Revelation seventeen, ...

> "I saw an eighth head, which is of the seven"? Rev 17:11

What does this mean?

Herein, we witness the beauty and precision of the Word of God. There can only be one answer to this question.

When the seventh head's fatal wound is healed, it comes back to life in a different capacity or expanded form.

How can the totality of the Beast, as represented by John's panoramic vision of the seven heads and ten horns (see Revelation 13), be concentrated into an eighth head?

> "And the beast that was, and is not, even he is the eighth, and is of the seven"(Revelation 17:11)

It is because this eighth is a Global World Empire. It is the synthesis and totality of all the preceding empires combined and concentrated into one head, the eighth head.

In the past, many theologians and others believed that the slain head was a man. During the 1960s, many thought that John Kennedy would perhaps have a satanic resurrection and be the revived head or the Antichrist. But it is clear that the heads on the Beast are empires, and these empires are depicted in symbolic form. Yet many still to this day confuse the Beast with the Antichrist. They are not one and the same!

The mystery of this scripture has stumped biblical scholars for centuries. Most of the missing information needed to solve the mystery was given in the last chapter, but there are some additional facts.

The death blow had to occur to fulfill prophecy. It was necessary for there to be a breakup of the limited world control accomplished by the British Empire.

It is highly unlikely that the world planners anticipated the degree to which Hitler got out of hand. Certainly the war worked to their advantage because it ended British world control. It took two world wars to do it.

**The Satanic Resurrection**

Warfare, specifically global world war, greatly benefits the money brokers. They derive terrific economic advantage by the financing of both the military buildup and then the urban renewal projects that come as a result of war's devastation. When the warring factions face the realities of rebuilding their countries, they must borrow large sums of money at usurious interest rates, thus bringing in great revenues to the international bankers.[1]

In this way, money is further concentrated into the hands of the banking elite, and the nations are weakened and brought into submission through debt. By instigating the wars and backing both sides, the bankers can't possibly lose. They win from both sides.

> "How art thou fallen from heaven, O Lucifer, son of the morning! how art thou cut down to the ground, which didst weaken the nations!"(Isaiah 14:12)

Most historians agree that the two world wars of the last century were actually one great war with several years of peace separating the two parts. If one were to study the elements that forged the beginning of World War I, it would be difficult to find a reason for why the whole world went to war in the first place. The fact of the matter is that there was no real cause for World War I to begin in 1914. Why then a war?

There were some interesting problems in Europe prior to the outbreak of hostilities in 1914. Europe could not afford to go to war simply because there was not enough mobilization of credit to enable the funding of the massive buildup necessary to finance such a venture.

The bankers in London solved the problem by contriving to set up a central banking system for the United States. Their agent, Paul Warburg, had been sent to develop the plan and have it formalized into law. The actual plan came to pass and became known as the Federal Reserve Act.[2]

Late in 1913, the United States Congress passed this act, which Woodrow Wilson rubber-stamped, centralizing the bank of the United States of America, and thus mobilizing the credit of the industrial giant. This mobilization of credit established the loaning capability to finance the First World War.

Eventually, the great world wars would bring to an end the seventh head of John's Beast, the British Empire. It was slain by a great sword, the world wars. Out of this would come the resurrected eighth head of the Beast, the final world empire.

> "And here is the mind which hath wisdom. The seven heads are seven mountains, on which the woman sitteth. And there are seven kings: five are fallen, and one is, and the other is not yet come; and when he cometh, he must continue a short space. And the beast that was, and is not, even he is the eighth, and is of the seven, and goeth into perdition." (Revelation 17:9-11)

**The Great Miracle Worker**

The resurrection of the slain head (into the eighth head) is accomplished by the capacity and work of the second Beast, or the False Prophet. The False Prophet resurrects the seventh head. He is the builder of the last great world empire, which would also have ten horns, as spoken of by Daniel.

The apostle John also saw ten horns on his rendition of the Beast. These horns are ten kings or kingdoms. While Daniel saw a little horn that proceeded out from the ten horns, John did not. This little horn grew larger than the ten horns (Daniel 7:20-24).

This little horn, which grows up larger (with the help of the False Prophet) than his ten compatriots, seems to represent the personification of a man who rules over the whole organism. The whole organism is encapsulated in John's vision as the eighth head that comes out of the seven (see Revelation 13).

The practical development of such a colossal edifice is by the effort of this second Beast. He finishes the age-old Beast system, bringing it to its final and completed form. In order for there to be an eighth head, the second Beast must be present and functioning, since it is through his miracle abilities that the New Global World Order will arise to completion at the end of the age.

## Chapter Twenty-One

# The Agent for the Anti-Christ

For two thousand years, Bible scholars have studied and wondered at the images of these two beasts of Revelation thirteen. Throughout the centuries, countless attempts have been made to identify each of these symbols as they relate to human history.

Now that we have moved through twenty centuries—some two thousand years since the birth of Christ—and six thousand years of recorded human history, most all the earth is expecting some kind of climactic event that will usher in the new millennium.

Since believers in Christ should be looking for His return soon, those within the commonwealth of faith should be reading the news carefully. History's unfolding events point to a clear understanding of what, and who, these symbolic creatures (Beasts) represent. The arising of both Beasts are signs that precede the return of Jesus Christ. The believer should be awake, looking intently to bolster his precious faith, and seeking the encrypted meaning of the Beast symbols.

The faithful are charged to warn the world of the coming trouble, and to open the eyes of those who cannot see.

These signs, though negative to the world, are actually good news because they point to Christ's return. God intended His prophetic Word to shine in the darkness, enabling those with a willing heart to see clearly the approaching of the day of the Lord. While even prophetic clarity tends to be fogged, the true disciples of Christ should be keen students of biblical prophecy and the signs of our day.

**The United Nations**

After the end of the Second World War, and the accompanying end of the British Empire (the seventh kingdom slain by the sword), the world was asleep as the eighth head, an eighth kingdom, emerged like a phoenix from the ashes of the ancient Roman Empire.

Scripture points out that this eighth head or empire will have ten kings or kingdoms combined in an alliance, and they will give their support to a world dictator. Scripture also teaches that this world dictator will be the False Christ, or the Antichrist.

**The Beast Emerges from the Sea**

The first Beast in Revelation thirteen slowly emerges from the sea into full view. These verses show that the revealing of that Beast will be gradual. It emerges from the sea. It is somewhat unnoticed, but then comes into full view.

In Daniel 8, we have a description of a little horn. First we see the little horn smaller than its contemporaries.

> "I considered the horns, and, behold, there came up among them another little horn." (Daniel 7:8)

Then we find that it grows larger than the ten horns, and finally it can be seen pulling three of those ten horns from their roots

> "And of the ten horns that were in his head, and of the other which came up, and before whom three fell; even of that horn that had eyes, and a mouth that spake very great things, whose look was more stout [larger in appearance] than his fellows." (Daniel 7:20)

Today, the greatest superpower in the world is the United States. A nation which was begun by a handful of folks arrived on the Mayflower from England, the smallest of nations, has now grown into the world's last and only superpower capable of uprooting nations.

It seems clear that in these last moments of human time, there is no other nation that seems to be able to challenge America's preeminence in the world today. Most likely, America is the little horn nation of Daniel, and we shouldn't be remiss to keep an eye on the presidency of the United States, or even former presidents who occupied that office.

When one stops to consider that the political apparatus for a Global World Empire (the United Nations) was developed and established here in the United States, the implications take on an ominous tone. In addition, the UN's present location on Manhattan Island in New York was bequeathed by the Rockefeller family, prominent international bankers.

This makes the emerging Beast rising from the sea even more like an elephant in the room—even to those that want to ignore its presence. The ten kings, however, remain to be seen.

As believers in prophecy rivet their attention on the more recent developments, they have inadvertently neglected the second Beast. There are two beasts mentioned in this very cryptic section of Scripture.

### What About the Second Beast?

It has been a mystery that has lurked in the shadow of the first Beast for thousands of years. Yet, it also appears at the end of the age along with the Global World Empire, the first Beast.

We now see the emerging Antichrist nation (United States) and the supra-structure of a world political body (United Nations) come into view, but what about the mysterious ten kings?

There are currently three possibilities:

1. The Common Market and its new monetary system, the Euro.
2. The Club of Rome's ten global federated economic zones
3. United States' ten economic zones set up under President Nixon.

As we see the eighth head emerging in these physical manifestations, the frightening reality is that the second Beast must be present on the earth. How so?

It is the second Beast whose function it is to advance and finish the final construction of the first Beast. And the final construction means the building of the eighth head.

Few realize that it is the two-horned Beast, the second Beast, which is contemporary with the final stages of the first Beast. He, or it, is the agent of the Antichrist, and is the architect who completes the entire Beast system.

If the rising of a World Global Government epicentered in the United Nations located in New York can be seen, then it stands to reason the second Beast must be in existence and functioning. It is he, according to Scripture, who finalizes the Beast system as he uses his three great powers to accomplish the great edifice.

The question remains, who, and what on the earth, is pulling all this together? Who is this second Beast of Revelation 13:11? What is the identity of this mysterious second Beast?

## Chapter Twenty-Two

# The False Prophet - the Second Beast

There are hidden clues which emerge from studying the first Beast that begin to unlock the identity of the second Beast. A return to a view of the first Beast is vital in discovering these facts.

As most students of prophecy already know, the first Beast of Revelation is also mentioned in Daniel (chapter 7). There is a significant difference, however, between what Daniel saw in his vision and what the apostle John saw in his vision. Both saw a final One World Government, but there was a difference in what each one saw. In that difference lies the first key in unlocking the mystery of the second Beast.

### Daniel's Vision

Daniel had a preview of the future, looking forward from his time to the end of the world. He saw the last phase or manifestation of the Beast system comprised of ten kings (Daniel 7:7).

He also saw a little horn, or king, with human eyes (Daniel 7:8). Daniel actually had a preview of the "man of lawlessness," the Antichrist. The Antichrist has also been called the world dictator who will control the ten nation confederacy. Daniel's vision was chronological—from his time forward, all the way to the last Global World Empire ruled by a man, the Antichrist.

**John's View**

John, on the other hand, saw panoramically. John, who lived in the first century, was given a total panoramic view of time. He was able to see from his time backward into history and forward into the future. His vision began with the Egyptian empire (around 2500 BC) all the way through time to the last days when the ten-horned kingdom that Daniel saw appears at the end of the age.

John saw a comprehensive panoramic and composite global world system that has been—and still is to this day—under construction, nearly five thousand years old (Revelation 13:1). Daniel merely saw the last form of that system in the last days, with the Antichrist coming to power at the end of the age. John in his vision does not give us any view of the Antichrist.

This is not to say that John didn't believe in the Antichrist. He, too, knew of the man of sin, but his vision on the island of Patmos did not reveal the Antichrist, only the Beast system(s).

Since John clearly saw the first Beast as a system, the pronoun "he" in the scripture pertains to the symbol that represents the system of the Beast. It is not speaking of some person (i.e. the Antichrist).

Rather, it pertains to the symbol: he, the Beast, the system; not he, the Beast, a man. Contextually, this gives us a precedent. The second Beast is also a system and not a person, as many have thought.

Since the second Beast is called the False Prophet, theologians assume it to be a man. It should not be thought of as an actual human being simply because the pronoun "he" is used; neither should we anthropomorphize the symbolism simply because of the terminology "the False Prophet."

In the case of the second Beast, as in the case of the first Beast, the pronoun relates to the symbol or the symbolism.

To bring clarity to the function of the second Beast he (or it) has been tagged the False Prophet because this entity gives out a misrepresentation of a religious idea. Pseudo prophetes is Greek for "false prophet."[1] This simply means "false messenger."

**Let There be Clarity**

Let there be clarity. First, there will be a man of lawlessness called the Antichrist. Second, there will be the Beast, which is a Global World Government system controlled and run by the Antichrist. The Beast is not the Antichrist, and the Antichrist is not the Beast. Third, there will be the False Prophet, or the second Beast, which is also a system, as we will see.

The three are distinct, but they are all related in spirit to serve only one purpose: to bring about a Global World Government and the worship of Lucifer on the earth.

The second Beast shows up on the world stage near the end of the age to finalize the construction of the New Global World Order, which includes the ten kings and the setting up of the Antichrist. This False Prophet appears at a point in time, specifically, after the healing of a fatal wound to one of the seven heads of the Beast as seen in Revelation 13:3. We have identified the seventh head or empire, as the British Empire.

The resurrected eighth head, evidenced in the United

Nations, arose out of the slain British Empire, through the collaborative effort of Great Britain and the United States.

The slain head, just to be very clear, has already been identified as the British Empire. It was Great Britain in collaboration with the United States that brought forth the eighth head of the Beast.

The "little horn" of Daniel—which starts out smaller then grows larger than the ten kings, and eventually rules over the ten— seems to fit the historical development of the United States. It began with ninety people and has become the only superpower on Earth today. The little horn, by its description in symbolic language, appears to be the synthesis of both a nation state and a man. The most powerful political office in the world today is the presidency of the United States. Please do not be confused between the two horned beast, the false prophet, and the little horn. They are both distinct.

America fits that description of the little horn that grew, but we still wait to see who the embodiment of the horn and how he embodied in a man. The ten kings are still yet unseen and seem to be future as well. They remain to be seen.

**Old Testament Foreshadows**

Old Testament types are used in Scripture to foreshadow a New Testament fulfillment. For example, the Ark of the Covenant carried by the Jewish priests was a foreshadowing of the believer. It is because the presence of God was in the ark, and today the presence of God comes to reside in human beings once they accept Christ Jesus and the subsequent receiving of the Holy Spirit. When faith is exercised they receive the Holy Spirit. God then dwells in humans when they receive His Spirit.

The parting of the Red Sea when God delivered the Hebrews

from Pharaoh was a type of water baptism, another example of these types.

The serpent raised in the wilderness was a foreshadowing of the cross. Jesus was the fulfillment of the Old Testament Passover lamb sacrificed by the Jews when they were slaves in Egypt.

Nevertheless, finding an Old Testament foreshadowing of the second Beast of Revelation thirteen presents difficulties.

The first Beast of Revelation is clearly foreshadowed in Daniel, and later John gives more light and detail on the subject. However, the second Beast is not so easily seen in the Old Testament.

There are some clues. John's vision of the first Beast as a system sets the tone and context for the interpretation of the second Beast as a system, but we must dig deeper for two more clues concerning the identity of the second Beast.

**The Two Horns**

> "And I beheld another beast coming up out of the earth; and he had two horns." (Revelation 13:11)

Scripture interprets Scripture, and it does not change to suit our subjective conjectural whims. Since the Scripture cannot change and is consistent throughout, if horns represent kings in one place, horns must represent kings in all places throughout apocalyptic Scripture.

> "The ram which thou sawest having two horns are the kings of Media and Persia." (Daniel 8:20)

If horns, as has been indicated, represent kings or kingdoms, the Beast with two horns in Revelation 13:11 represents two kings or two kingdoms that combine to make a system that is called and represented as the False Prophet.

It has been said that there is vague reference in the Old Testament to shed light on the second Beast in Revelation thirteen. But there is some light to focus on.

There is a two horned beast mentioned in the book of Daniel. Those two horns a clearly identified as the two kingdoms of Media and Persia. They are explained as a two-horned beast. Thus, Daniel 8:3 lays down an Old Testament precedent for a two-nation alliance depicted in symbolism as a two-horned beast.

Interpreting the False Prophet as a solitary man would not take into consideration the two horns in light of biblical precedents.

**The Alliance of Two Kings**

The false prophet is an alliance of two kingdoms. It is a system.

> "And he had two horns like a lamb, and he spake as a dragon" (Ibid)

In the Old Testament, the Scripture, as recorded through the prophet Daniel, describes the Gentile world powers as beasts.

The figurative language Daniel uses to describe the ruling powers actually contains the characteristics of those ruling nations. For example, Daniel saw the Babylonian Empire as a lion, the king of the jungle. This indicated the regal power of Nebuchadnezzar and the greatest of all civilizations. He saw the second empire as a bear, which described the characteristics of the Medes and Persians. The Medo-Persian Empire was known for its sheer power and weight in numbers of people.

The Grecian Empire he characterized as a leopard, cunning and swift, always stalking the prey and moving quickly over the land. This is exactly how Alexander the Great operated. The fourth beast, Rome, was different than the others. It seemed to be a mechanical and heartless system.

These little cameos of the former empires in symbolic form are mentioned here only to bring light and embellishment upon the imagery and interpretation of the second Beast, as it is also described in a symbolic form.

**The Lamb like Appearance of the False Prophet**

The second Beast is described as lamb-like in appearance. A lamb in the Bible is first mentioned in the life of Abel (Genesis 4:4).

The age-old story records that when Abel went to worship, he took a lamb from his flock and sacrificed it to the Lord. This sacrifice was acceptable to the Lord, and it was a foreshadowing of Christ, the Lamb of God.

When God was testing Abraham's obedience, He required a lamb as a substitutionary sacrifice for Abraham's son, Isaac (Genesis 22:8). The ancient Jews were also required to sacrifice a lamb and paint the blood of the lamb on the lintel of the door, escaping the judgment that was coming down on Egypt (Genesis 12:3; Exodus 12:21-23). In all these cases, a lamb was a foreshadowing of Christ.

The False Prophet, or the second Beast, is false because it represents itself as Christ-like (thus, the characterization as a lamb). Yet, in reality, underneath the veneer it is satanic—it speaks like a dragon, a wolf in sheep's clothing.

Remember, this second Beast is a two-nation alliance, or

system. If the lamb symbol is a Christian symbol, then the two kingdoms, or horns, represent two Christian nations, or two nations that are at least considered Christian nations:

They have a Christian pretense or appearance, but underneath it there resides a darkness. The fact that it "speaks as a dragon" explains that beneath the Christian pretense hides the devil: a liar, a thief, and a murderer.

The second Beast, then, is a system of two alleged Christian nations joined together to form an alliance, who by their external appearance (look like a lamb, i.e., Christian) give out a deceiving message or impression.

What two nations, which have banded together to build a One World Global System for the seat of Antichrist, could this be talking about? Before this question can be answered, there are additional facts that must be uncovered.

**The Sphere of the Authority of the False Prophet**

> "And he exercised all the power of the first beast before him, and causeth the earth and them which dwell therein to worship the first beast, whose deadly wound was healed." (Revelation 13:12)

This next section of Scripture is critical in destroying vain speculations concerning the identity of the False Prophet. Hopefully, the Scripture by itself will put to an end and bury those annoying conjectures.

The key words are "he" and "all": "he exercises all the authority of the first Beast." This statement is very revealing. One must ask the very important question, "If the False Prophet exercises all the authority of the first Beast, just what is the extent of the authority of the first Beast?"

The word "authority" used here is the Greek word exousia, means "legislative authority" or "licensing authority."[2]

The False Prophet has all the licensing legal authority of the first Beast. This is a great deal more than mere religious authority, as we shall see. Just what is (and has been) the comprehensive authority of this five-thousand-year-old Beast system?

The Beast with the ten horns—and the seven heads, as you will recall—was a symbolic representation of all the empires that controlled the world from the time of the Egyptians to this present day. The fundamental controlling authority of those empires worked over the spheres of politics, economics, law, military, education, and to a great degree, even religion.

Think of the power of Egypt, Babylon, Greece, and Rome. Think of the British Empire and its navy, its commercial life, its state-run religion, and its banking power. The False Prophet operates with all the power of the first Beast: all the authority and power, all the spheres and dimensions of an empire.

Think of the power he wields. How would it be to have all power over the Western world's political, economic, legal, military, educational, and religious arenas of life?

The important point to be made here, in no uncertain terms, is that this is not just some religious entity moving with a new religious order of some sort.

The False Prophet's power extends far beyond the sphere of the religious dimension. This second Beast moves with all authoritative legal power.

## He is Contemporary

> "And he exercised all the power of the first beast before him [in his presence]. (Revelation 13:12)

The phrase "in his presence" shows us that the two entities

are contemporary—that they appear together—but the authority of the False Prophet has not been initially received from the first Beast. It seems as though both of the entities have the same authoritative power source. The first Beast seems indifferent towards the authority of the False Prophet. He doesn't seem to be intimidated by the False Prophet's power. They work together to produce the final result.

In a moment we shall see the operation of the False Prophet's comprehensive authority. These facts are important because they help to acquire a greater objectivity concerning just who and what is the False Prophet.

**To Recapitulate the facts of the False Prophet:**

- The second Beast is a two-horned system, or a two-nation confederacy.
- He will function during a period when the seventh head of the first Beast has been healed from a fatal wound of war (a great sword). That is he is contemporary with the first Beast's last phase of completion.
- He will have all the power (legal authority) of the first Beast.

**The False Prophet also does great signs:**

- He will have power to call fire down from heaven.
- He will be able to deceive the whole world, particularly through an image.
- He will abolish all economic systems where cash is used as the medium of exchange and introduce a cashless system that will operate through 666 (see Revelation 13:12-18).

These great signs and wonders that the second Beast performs will be dealt with in more detail in later chapters, but all these great powers are at his disposal to finalize the construction of the last great Global World System.

It is a great mistake to assign to the False Prophet the small task of merely building a new, worldwide religion. As we have shown, his power extends far beyond religious confusion and deception.

## When Shall These Things Be?

Today, many believe that these manifestations of the powers of the second Beast will occur at a point in the future. Could it be that they are already in operation today?

The discussion of this topic will cause great pain to many people. It calls into question one's pre-suppositional position on biblical prophecy (eschatology—the study of last things) and, therefore, one's approach to the book of Revelation.

## Looking at Book of Revelation

Basically there are four known schools of thought for the interpretation of the book of Revelation.

1. The spiritual scheme: The Apocalypse is given to teach fundamental spiritual principles.
2. The preterist scheme: The book only teaches events taking place on earth during the Roman era, during the time of the apostle John's life.
3. The historic scheme: The symbols in Revelation relate to events in the history of the world that are relevant to the welfare of the church from the first century to modern times.
4. The futurist scheme: This view insists that, for the most part, the visions of the book will be future, toward the end of the age.

The question one has to ask is, which of the above views is accurate? That is, which set of spectacles should be used?

There has been constant debate on this problem for hundreds of years, and the believer is left to ferret it out for himself. Each point of view has merits. In the North American church, the prominent view, by and large, is the futurist scheme.

The futurist scheme, for the most part, insists that the visions of Revelation will be fulfilled toward the end of the age. While there may be a great deal of truth to this position, it also creates its own problem. The problem with "futurism" is that the closer we move toward the end of the age, the more likely we are to overlook and miss the events predicted in the symbols and assign their fulfillment to some future time. This view keeps pushing the fulfillment of events ahead into the future so that we never arrive.

As fantastic as it may seem, a careful study of history will show that the False Prophet has been with us for some time, and that he is alive and in the world today.

## Chapter Twenty-Three

# The New Zion

For most of them, it began as an escape from feudalism and the despotism that reigned over their religious lives. England and Europe were basically without a middle class.The average person had no hope of ever holding land. All property was considered owned by the king and was controlled by the very rich. The rest of the people were serfs.[1] This was called feudalism. In England, the reigning king also dictated the nature of worship to God. Christianity was tightly controlled by the sovereign king.[2]

Those in England who continued to dream of freedom deeply desired a fresh start. They were willing to brave the difficulties and harshness of the journey to the New World.

The ones that finally did venture out believed they were coming to the New Jerusalem, the Promised Land. Their escape from England was looked at spiritually. They saw it as an exodus from an Egypt. But they also viewed their awaited liberties in the new land with a prophetic sense of purpose.[3]

**A Fresh Start**

These visionaries had first-hand knowledge of the terrible bondage of feudalism and despotism. They saw the possibility in the new land as the potential fulfillment of all their hopes and dreams—a new nation (America) based upon the Judeo-Christian law and morality from the sacred Scriptures.

In the beginning there was a terrible price to be paid as they carved out a niche in the hostile world, but to them it was a small price as they considered the great opportunity and the potential that lay before them.[4]

**The Exodus**

It started out as resistance to the Anglican Church. The religious oppression under the state-run church eventually became so intolerable that those who had deep-seated convictions about God had to leave.

They were the separatists, and they moved across the English Channel to the mainland of Europe to a place of refuge in Holland. After spending eleven years there, in exile from England, the hearts of these zealots still longed for a new kind of freedom. The exhausting toil of eighteen-hour workdays for meager wages was straining their sensibilities. Why not break free and move to the New World in America?[5]

As a devout and religious people, they took counsel through corporate prayer. They believed that their God was inspiring them to brave the elements and trust Him for a new beginning in a far away land.[6] About a hundred of them crowded into the Mayflower—a ship roughly the size of a volleyball court—and for sixty-six days braved the awesome power of the mighty Atlantic Ocean.[7]

One year after landing at Plymouth Rock, almost half of

the valiant band had already starved to death. The Thanksgiving celebration later that year was the beginning of an American tradition memorializing their heroic faith in God.[8]

The lords of England on the other side of the Atlantic Ocean viewed the colonists as rebels. Like Pharaoh of Egypt, they would not let the people go to the land of promise without contest. Elitist elements within Britain sought to retain control and subdue the colonies. The new land, it was reasoned, must be kept under British control.[9]

## The Bank of England Interruption

In America in 1692, Massachusetts opened a mint and began to issue its own coins and, later, paper notes. These notes were considered full legal tender. The notes could be borrowed at low interest rates by the citizens for all sorts of needs: business, homes, etc. The revenues that came from these low-interest loans were used for public purposes and thus kept taxes down. This was all done without the consent of England. Other colonies followed the lead of Massachusetts and enjoyed great prosperity. The colonies paid no interest and therefore were not indebted to anyone.[10]

In England, however, King William III made a decision to give William Paterson and his associates a charter to establish a private bank. It was called the Bank of England.[11]

The king needed money to finance his war with France. This favor was extended in exchange for the loan. The bank had the exclusive privilege of issuing paper money and lending it at interest. With control of London and England's monetary system now in hand, the bankers fixed their gaze on the New World, intensely motivated and determined to control its currency as well.[12]

By 1720, every colonial governor was instructed to stop issuing their own paper notes. The bankers in England slyly used the British Board of Trade as their front, thus manipulating the Parliament and affecting decisions so that the English government would back their movements against the American colonies. The colonies refused to submit. The conflict that later boiled over and became the American Revolution was under way, but the seed of that armed conflict was the control of money.[13]

During 1767, Ben Franklin tried to fiscally conciliate the colonies with the Crown Empire, but Franklin's diplomacy did not work. While Franklin was in England, former Prime Minister Granville spoke to the House of Commons. His words became the guidance system for international banking.

"I will tell the honorable gentlemen of a revenue that will produce something valuable in America. Make paper money for the colonies [under British control], issue it upon loan there, take the interest and apply it as you think proper." [14]

Since the English government also held this underhanded vision, it backed the Bank of England to the hilt. Therefore, the bank was ready to apply and enforce their policy of monetary control over the American colonies.

It should be crystal clear that the intent of this policy was to enslave the New World in and through debt. The colonies resisted this fiscal tyranny and met on June 10, 1775. There they resolved to create two million dollars in bills of credit that the united colonies would honor. This action was viewed by the British as open defiance and rebellion. The boiling point had been reached. The explosive social condition erupted in what came to be known as the "Boston Tea Party." This was the event that launched the Revolutionary War. The momentum for the war, however, had begun building some eighty years earlier.[15]

## The Boston Tea Party

The Boston Tea Party and the American Revolution expressed the deeply entrenched sentiments of those who yearned to be free from the domination of the British Empire.

What the patriots were saying, as they dumped the tea into Boston Harbor, was that they were fed up with being taxed, fed up with having no control of their own credit, and fed up with the struggle over the printing of their own nation's money.[16]

Through taxation, the Americans essentially were paying to be policed by a power they didn't want ruling over them. This was their initial reason for the exodus from Britain. The British had cunningly extorted from the colonies money that was being used to garrison British troops on American soil. They did this to maintain a watchful eye on the colonies. The war for independence was over a whole lot more than a little tax on tea.

Although the escape to the New World was, to a great extent, a religious matter, the Revolutionary war was fought over taxation and, more importantly, who would control capital/ money in the New World.

## The Rothschilds

The Rothschilds, a family of Jewish lineage, were very shrewd in their dealings with money. They gained large sums of capital by investment and later became international bankers. Five sons of Rothschild dispersed to continental Europe and set up banking houses in strategic locations in various European countries.[17]

Around 1799, the Rothschilds, with increased financial power, allied themselves with the Masonic secret societies. Under cover of obscurity, they successfully destabilized the European continent by financing the French Revolution. London became the seat of the Rothschilds' international banking dynasty.[18]

The Rothschilds and other banking families were secretly establishing new power centers, while the dynastic monarchies of Europe were disintegrating. The influence of the bankers was exerted on both businesses and governments.[19]

The fledgling America presented an obstacle to the schemes for British world control held by the monetary interests. The new nation continued to refuse the shackles of a central bank, and America's credit remained relatively free from foreign control. Since lending power in America was not in the hands of the international manipulators, the bankers were frustrated in proceeding with their global aspirations.[20]

The fundamental concept these international pirates used in their business practice came from a promise in the Old Testament, which they twisted in their application to themselves.

> "Thou shalt lend unto many nations, but thou shalt not borrow; and thou shalt reign over many nations, but they shall not reign over thee" (Deuteronomy 15:6).

The Rothschilds built on this principle, but they subverted the scriptural intent and, instead, lent money at usurious rates. They believed that if they controlled the wealth of a nation, they could transcend and usurp the legal and political power of the state. Rothschild would often boast, "I care not who makes the laws of a nation, give me the wealth of a nation and I'll make the laws."[21] They conducted themselves along the lines of the blueprint for world control mapped out in the Protocols of the Illuminati.[22]

**Adam Weishaupt-the Illuminati**

Adam Weishaupt was a professor of considerable renown at

Ingolstadt University. He was driven by an incredible, diabolical ambition to rule the world. Unlike others throughout history who sought the same prize, Weishaupt was not a crude gangster sort who could lead a band of thieves and rowdies. Neither was he a military type who sought conquest through sheer force. Weishaupt was an intellectual, a professor at law. His high-minded self-conceit caused him to believe he was mentally superior to all others. He was received into the Masonic Order of his day, where he found like-minded comrades.[23]

Those who banded together with Weishaupt felt they were of such superior fiber that they should be running the world. A secret order was devised called the Illuminati, which would become the vehicle for world conquest.[24]

**The Scope of the Illuminati**

The Order of the Illuminati sought to unite men from all places, all social classes, and all religions, despite the diversity of their opinions and passions. The idea was to make them love the common interest of unity and bond to the point where, together or alone, they act as one individual.

The ultimate objective was to bring happiness to the world. Thus, from this motive came the battle cry of the French Revolution "liberty, equality, fraternity." But behind the deceptive slogan was an evil motive. Most likely, these three words are the three frogs or evil spirits that proceed out of the mouth of the False Prophet.

> "And I saw three unclean spirits like frogs come out of the mouth of the dragon, and out of the mouth of the beast, and out of the mouth of the false prophet." (Revelation 16:13)

The slogan of the liberals "liberty, equality, and fraternity," was a deceptive humanitarian ruse that appealed to the masses but a deceitful lie. It is the same mantra chanted by progressives in the streets of America and around the world.

The philosophy behind this was the rather novel and twisted logic that the end—happiness for the people— justified the means.[25]

The ultimate purpose of the Illuminati, however, was to take over the world.

Talent for the Order was processed by an elaborate system of initiation. The initiate would have to pass from one degree to the next, with the goal being the completion of all the steps to full enlightenment. Weishaupt carefully plotted each step of the way, making sure the weakest would not rise above the lowest levels of the Order. The bold, ruthless, and cynical were brought along to the highest levels of Reagent, Magus, and Rex.[26]

**Illuminism and Freemasonry**

Weishaupt believed that his organization needed a cover and a way to extend its power. In 1782, he successfully infiltrated the Masonic Order with Illuminism at the Congress of Wilhelmsbad.[27]

In America, George Washington, who was a Freemason, became aware of the movements of the Illuminati within the Masonic Order. A Christian minister gave Washington a book entitled, Proofs of a Conspiracy. This was Washington's response to the book.

"It was not my intention to doubt that the doctrines of the Illuminati, and principles of Jacobinism, had not spread to the United States. On the contrary, no one is more fully satisfied of this fact than I am. The idea that I meant to convey was that I did not believe the Lodges of Freemasonry in this country had, as societies, endeavored to propagate the diabolical tenets of the Illuminati."[28]

For the Order to gain its objective, it was necessary to abolish religion, governments, and private property. The Order deemed these the real obstacles to true happiness. This is exactly what the Communists have been advocating since 1848. But most importantly, the Illuminati, and later the Communists, advocated the centralization of credit in the hands of the state by means of a national bank with state capital and an exclusive monopoly.[29]

In Europe, the Order of the Illuminati was driven underground when its plans were discovered. However, the ideas, the plans, and the goals—of John Ruskin, Cecil Rhodes, Rothschild, the Round Table, the CFR, the Bilderbergers, and Masonry— have lived on in the Communist movement.

**The British Spy System**

The British never conceded America's declared independence as the final inning in British world hegemony. Their aims of world dominion would not be frustrated by a few farmers and wild-eyed dreamers on the other side of the Atlantic.

In the late eighteenth century in the United States, two prominent political figures squared off in a duel to the death. The gun-fight is but a faint memory in the minds of most observers of history, but the reasons for the hostilities between these two famous historic personalities lies buried in the rubble of time. The battle to the death involved Alexander Hamilton, who became known as the father of the American banking system, and Aaron Burr, vice president of the United States.[30]

The story is somewhat a mystery, but it provides a key to

unlocking important facts concerning Great Britain's continuous struggle to regain control of America. America's economic development is directly related to Britain's (the bankers of London) attempts to seize this nation.

Through this study it can be seen why today the citizens of this land are buried in mountainous debt and thus monumental taxation: They are the same issues that brought about the American Revolution in the first place.

Since it was costly and difficult to maintain a war effort in the Western world—especially with Europe in turmoil from the outburst of the French Revolution—the British intelligence sent spies into the United States with the intent of seizing the country from within.

Their chief man of the hour was Rothschild's agent, Aaron Burr. Burr was a fully trained agent of the British internationalists. Most importantly, Burr was a Scottish Rite Freemason of the 33rd degree (the Illuminati infiltrated Scottish Rite Freemasonry). Here, in the person of Aaron Burr, can be seen the synthesis of the intent of both the world bankers and the Illuminati Scottish Rite Freemasonry.[31]

After becoming governor of New York, Burr helped obtain cheap loans for the internationalists to buy up most of New York State. Burr helped found the Manhattan Bank (the Chase Manhattan Bank—now the J.P. Morgan Chase Manhattan Bank), and much has been written about his nefarious dealings in the South as he helped lay the groundwork for the Civil War in the first decade of the 1800s.[32]

When Burr sought to become president of the United States, he was frustrated by Alexander Hamilton, who viewed him as a traitor. Burr was also highly suspected by George Washington. History documents Burr's family ties with Benedict Arnold, the most infamous traitor in American history.[33]

When he ran for president, Burr was narrowly defeated by Jefferson. Had it not been for Hamilton, the Rothschilds' agent Aaron Burr would have become president of the United States of America. There is much behind the duel that most history books do not tell us, but the most important fact is yet to come.

**The Bank of the U.S.A.**

Alexander Hamilton is known today as the father of the American banking system. Even though Hamilton was a red-blooded American, he wanted a central bank (modeled after the French ideal). The French ideal was simply that certain prominent, successful, and intelligent men would control the affairs of the bank. Jefferson was against the charter of such a bank, fearing too much power in the hands of an elitist group. Even though these men were Americans, Jefferson felt it was still too dangerous a proposition.

Burr also wanted a central bank, but his bank would have internationalists as those in command. Burr killed Hamilton and fled to Britain. At issue was who would control money in the New World, the British banking system or an American group.

While Burr was vice president, he and Albert Gallatin (another internationalist who had become secretary of the treasury), successfully sold the idea of the need for a balanced budget to Congress. By cutting military expenditures for the maintenance of the U.S. Navy, the defenses of the United States were weakened. This undermining of U.S. defenses opened the door for the British to stage another conflict.[34]

The second revolutionary war (in 1812) was orchestrated by the Trojan horse of the British spy system that had infiltrated American politics. The second revolutionary war should have ended what Europeans called "the American experiment," but to the exasperation of the British bankers, the war failed. There is no explanation for America's survival except to see it as an intervention of providence.[35]

**The Civil War: Battle with the Bankers**

By the time Abraham Lincoln became president, the United States had survived two revolutionary wars with Great Britain, as well as many political intrigues, especially during Andrew Jackson's administration. The pesky child nation, America, was causing great delay to the global aspirations of the British Empire. After the failure to recharter the bank of the United States, the European bankers began plotting another war.

During Lincoln's administration, the British inspired the Civil War. The war itself would create the need to finance the war through borrowing. The plotters realized the American people would not accept a national bank without a reason for having one. They decided upon a war. Wars are costly, and they force governments into a position in which they must borrow to finance the effort.

Who could the plotters induce to fight in a war with America? Since America had become such a powerful nation, there was no one to rival her in the western hemisphere. No one.

The bankers made the decision to divide the nation into two parts, thereby creating an enemy from within the United States. The overt issue for the war was slavery, but the actual reason behind the Civil War was the splitting of the Union. The deeper motive was, of course, to seize control of the country by creating the financial need to borrow from the bankers at usurious interest rates, thus creating the need for a centralized bank.[36]

The whole story of the secession of the southern states was

given by George L. Bickley, who declared that he created the fateful war of 1861. He worked through an organization called the Knights of the Golden Circle, which engineered and spread secession.[37]

**The British Bankers Lending Control**

The British bankers at that time also controlled the fledgling American banks which offered to loan Abraham Lincoln money to fight the war. Lincoln wisely refused and created the famous Lincoln greenbacks with which he financed the Civil War.[38]

Abraham Lincoln, in a famous address, declared:

"At what point, then, is the approach of danger to be expected? I answer, if it ever reach us it must spring up among us, it cannot come from abroad. If destruction be our lot, we must ourselves be its author and finisher. As a nation of freemen we must live through all time or die of suicide." [39]

Lincoln's refusal to finance the Union through debt to the internationalists demonstrated his keen insight into their strategy for global dominion. Hence, he financed the Civil War by printing the Lincoln greenbacks.

In both respects—with regard to the Civil War and the British bankers' attempt to seize control of the economics of America—once again the aims of the globalists were frustrated. This is what caused Lincoln's assassination.

Nonetheless, America remained in control of her own credit. The result of this victory was low interest loans for entrepreneurs, which led to great business expansion.

This great expansion in the post-Civil War era enhanced the fears of those who sought to bring the world into a One World Order. If America was allowed to continue to expand, she would be a major—perhaps insurmountable—obstacle in the way of their goal.

For one hundred years, America was able to avoid total control of her capital by the international bankers. Lincoln was most certainly a great irritant and obstacle to the aspirations of the globalists. He was the last president to seek categorically a halting of the globalists' drive toward a Global One World Government. It cost him his life; he was murdered by John Wilkes Booth, also an agent of the internationalists.[40]

America's emergence from the Civil War as a great industrial power was due to the effective centralization of capital and credit within the Federal Government, thanks to Lincoln. It was America's control over her own capital that was making her prosperous. It was the aim of the international bankers to change all that.

Lincoln was the victim of a major conspiracy—a conspiracy so important that even the European bankers were involved.

Lincoln had to be eliminated because he dared to oppose their attempt to force a central bank on the United States. He became an example to those who would later oppose such machinations in high places.

Could it be that, one hundred years later, John F. Kennedy succumbed to the same fate and was also a victim of the same intrigue?

## Chapter Twenty-Four

# The Post-Civil War Era

It became crystal clear to the globalists, after the American Civil War, that America had to be stopped. Frederick Engels, the British industrialist, was one of many who felt that the war would be the end of the American republic. The victory of the North proved him wrong. Now, the tremendous threat of the American system loomed an even greater shadow over the vast British Empire and continental Europe. A more vigorous strategy was plotted and pursued to finally overthrow England's rebellious child, now almost one hundred year old.

A plan to counter the great American expansion had to be conceived. A new economic warfare would be waged.

The plan for this overthrow centered again on the nation's money and credit. This was done by forces inside the United States contracting U.S. currency (greenbacks) and lowering tariff barriers so that American markets could be exploited. Low tariffs meant that American industry would not be protected from foreign competition.

This clandestinely contrived free trade policy would exploit the markets of America and suck money away from circulation in the States. In other words, in the eyes of the British, the greenbacks had to go because they kept their own bankers from being in control.

Then, the international pirates sought to bring about reform by replacing industry builders with foreign agents in seats of economic and political power. In order to conquer America, her financial sovereignty must, of necessity, come to an end. This became the sole front of the internationalists in their pursuit for a One World Global Government.[1]

**English Economic Counterattack**

The internationalists refused to be deterred. Neither the American Revolution, nor the second revolutionary war, nor the failure of the re-chartering of the bank, nor the failure of the Civil War could frustrate their aspirations. They never ceased to work to subjugate and recapture America. However, a new strategy was planned. The British intelligence, under the control of the internationalists, sought to undermine the new nation from deep within.Conspirators were sent to the United States to assail the greenbacks. The English-backed Golden Club was implanted in the eastern United States for the sole purpose of throttling the successes of Lincoln's economic policies. After much wrangling and dissimulation, restrictions were placed upon the greenbacks.[2]

The bankers fought hard against the American government's attempt to recapture its own credit and money. They emerged from their war on Lincoln's greenbacks with the prize.

The restrictions that were placed upon the greenbacks caused a perception that made them inflationary. The bankers, with clever manipulation, were able to expand and contract the economy. They would not accept the greenbacks in payment for lands they had bought from the government. They demanded gold. For many years, there was a general looting of the government's gold, and the huge banking house of J.P. Morgan was built as an international banking island upon the American soil.[3]

During the administration of Abraham Lincoln, the powerful London-based banking house of Rothschild was behind the efforts to throttle the control of—and to seize—credit and money in America. In a letter to Mr. Belmont, Rothschild warned of ruin for those who might oppose the payment of U.S. bonds in coin or who might advocate their liquidation in greenbacks.[4]

**Ideological War and Political Intrigue**

Frederick Engels was a brilliant British industrialist whose business depended greatly on cheap American slave cotton. Engels, who was the most famous of all British industrialists, paid great homage to the East India House think tank. The mind trust included men like Thomas Carlyle, John Stuart Mill, Thomas Malthus, and Charles Darwin—all of whom had great influence on Engels. Their political economic socialist ideas, based upon feudalism, became Engels' launching pad for his development of the ideology of communism. Frederick Engels was the founder of Marxist communism and author of its doctrine. He was a personal mentor to Karl Marx.

What was most greatly feared by the British internationalists was beginning to truly threaten their plans for entire global control. America and her nation-building republican system was being brought to the mainland of Europe by Germany. It was being accomplished by Friedrich List, who had been sent to America to study the American system.[5]

List, after watching the success of the American republican model, believed it was his duty and responsibility to promote everything that may increase the wealth and power of the nation. Tariffs must be erected to protect fledgling industry from nations that would attempt to loot by bringing cheaper goods. List saw the evil of free trade.[6]

The British imperial system was the antithesis of the free trade British ideal. Those in control knew the advantages of a free trade system and its power to maintain both the expansion of its own economy and overall world control.

As the thrust of the American system's influence grew and was introduced to Germany, a secret British offensive was launched against these neo-German republicans and Abraham Lincoln's economic program in the United States.

It was in 1843 that Frederick Engels, father of communism, entered the fray. In his first treatise on economics, he attacked Christianity (the base of the American republican system) and carefully directed his readers to the free trade versus protectionist battle then going on in Germany. He pointed out how essential it was to follow the position of free trade as the "proper course of action" and "the shorter road to wealth."[7]

Engels, after winning over Karl Marx, published their first co-authored book, The Condition of the Working Class. The book served as a false prophetic warning to the German working class of the horrors in store for them if (energized by America) imported industrialization developed.[8]

Marx then teed off on Frederick List through his book, The National System of Political Economy; he branded List as a propagator of the special interests of German manufacturers.

The titanic battle between the ideologies of republicanism and feudalism stymied the industrialization and unification of Germany until the latter part of the nineteenth century. As the Engels/Marx communist duet was gaining the upper hand in slowing the growth of mainland European industrialization, they used the same fear inspired by these literary weapons for international globalism.

Lincoln's greenbacks mobilized national credit in America and thus financed the victory of the North in the Civil War. Had Lincoln surrendered to the temptation of the bankers' loans (with exorbitant interest rates), the borrower (the U.S.A.) would have become slave to the lender (England). Lincoln saw the evils of both the free trade ideology and the slavery system that supported cheap cotton for England's textile mills, which allowed them to maintain a tremendous economic edge over the rest of the world.[9]

Britain, in control of raw materials, could not only bring the cotton to England and then back to America, but all over the world. If ever these nations were to industrialize and manufacture their own finished products, they could erect trade barriers and destroy the monopoly that the British enjoyed over these worldwide markets.

Here, the ideological mixture of communism and British free trade expansionism was the not-so-strange brew that was created to stifle the Christian-based republicanism of American design.

As a result, it successfully stifled the advancement of industrialization to the European continent which could have enabled nations to break out of feudalist indentured slavery.[10]

The Communist movement was one of a number of political weapons created by British strategists to counter the spread of the tremendously successful American system to the European continent.

**Britain's Conquest of Mammon- The Rothschilds' War Chest for Globalism**

In the late nineteenth and early twentieth centuries, with the American purse falling more and more into the hands of the international banking elite, the final conflict to set up the hundred-year-old Illuminati plan for an American central bank was staged.

As the internationalists orchestrated the depression of 1907, the American populace was finally psychologically prepared to receive a centralized banking plan. It was a plan that promised to control and stabilize the flow of capital. The plan called for a central bank that was promised to be run by the government.

It would be a bank that would regulate cash flows with the promise that there would never again be a shortage of money in circulation. It would ensure that there would always be sufficient money, the lifeblood of an economy, flowing in the economy. It was a lie!

**Great Deception**

The international planners knew—oh, how they knew—that the American people would never accept a plan that could possibly allow private interests to control the bank. The American people wanted a bank that was controlled by the government, not by private banking houses like the Rothschilds and the J.P. Morgans.

"I care not who makes the laws of the nations. Give me the wealth of the nations and I'll make the laws". Rothschild [12]

Under a cloak of great secrecy, the plotters of world financial and governmental control retreated to a place called

Jekyll Island. There they plotted and schemed and created, with great subtlety, the Federal Reserve Act. The Rothschilds sent their special agent, Paul Warburg, to head up the delegation. His mission was to stage the takeover and set up the American banking system.

**Jekyll Island**

Warburg called together the most powerful and wealthy families in America. Then, with their support, he drafted two infamous plans that laid the groundwork for the seizure of the American banking system. Actually, there was just one plan with two different names.

At Jekyll Island, the representatives of these powerful families made agreements that framed the diabolical plot. Plan one was called the Aldrich Plan. Plan two was called the Federal Reserve Act. History records which one of these identical plans was accepted by the U.S. Congress.[13]

**The Federal Reserve**

The Federal Reserve Act created what became the central bank of the United States of America: the Federal Reserve System.

Contrary to popular understanding, the Fed is not controlled by the U.S. government but by representatives who are selected by the international bankers themselves.[14] The Fed's decision-making processes reminds one of the fox who guarded the chicken house.

Unbeknownst to the American public, the Federal Reserve System is a private corporation that in 1913, by craft and guile, became the American banking system. Actually, the name Federal Reserve was given for the express purpose of deceiving the populace into thinking it was a government agency. It is not.[15]

George Washington, the father of this country, spoke these words of wisdom concerning the formation of a central bank.

"Shall a few designing men, for their own aggrandizement, and to glorify their own avarice, overset the goodly fabric we have been rearing at the expense of much time, blood and treasure?"[16]

Father George saw the evil desire of the international bankers and what they sought to accomplish with a central bank. This statement by George Washington caused the founding fathers to carefully craft into the Constitution to the United States Congress the specially assigned powers of Congress to include:

Congress shall have the power to coin money and regulate the value thereof.[17]

The purpose for this delegation of authority to Congress was to specifically prevent robbery and exploitation of the American money system by a select few. The Federal Reserve Act was passed on December 23,1913, Woodrow Wilson refused to veto the passage of the bill by Congress.

The passage of the Federal Reserve bill took away the legal authority of Congress to have the power to coin money and regulate the value thereof, and it gave this power to a private printing company called the Federal Reserve. Basically, what this meant was that the Fed could print money and charge interest. The revenues derived from that interest would accrue to the personal benefit of the principal stockholders of the Federal Reserve (corporation) System.

This is exactly what Thomas Jefferson feared, what Abraham Lincoln opposed, and what George Washington warned of. The victory for which the founding patriots gave their lives during the Revolutionary War had been simply handed over to those they so valiantly fought against.

The Federal Reserve Act was passed on December 23, 1913, while most of the Congress was home for Christmas. But what did the plan allow for? The very thing Aaron Burr sought one hundred years earlier: a central bank in the United States controlled by the international bankers from London.

The banking privilege, which had been sought after for so long, was now finally in the hands of the globalists. The seizure of the money-making privilege, and the control of credit by the bank, guaranteed the necessary power to establish the funding instrument for an inevitable Global World Government. The ability to expand and contract credit was securely in the hands of the internationalists. Now they had the ability to centralize and concentrate capital into the hands of an elite group that could control the world.

Over the last one hundred-some years, the sinister brilliance of the Fed has looted the American people and created enormous national debt. The ability for it to create fiat money (money not backed by silver or gold) by simply making a notation in a ledger created great inflationary forces and led to the creation of the graduated income tax.

The internationalists also have controlling interests in munitions companies and reap huge profits from war. Governments must buy from them to fight the wars that the internationalists create.

The borrowing nations must then promise to pay back the capital needed for their war machines by issuing promissory notes called bonds. The greatest borrower of these funds is America. The combined debt of the world does not equal the amount of borrowed capital that America owes in issued bonds.

The government can make these pledges (bonds) of repayment to the Fed because the people of the United States yearly pay their taxes (graduated taxes) which guarantee repayment. These massive yearly revenues have come under the control of the Fed.

**The Conquest of America**

When America finally lost control of her money, she gave up financial freedom. It can be said that when America lost control of her money, she was ostensibly recaptured by Britain—or, more specifically, by those who control Britain.

Very slowly, almost without perception, America has become and is becoming a socialized nation. The manipulation of our monetary system by the creation of debt and the necessity for high taxes is creating a situation where more and more freedom is being taken away and lost. This phenomenon is eliminating the middle class and creating a neo-feudalism.

The average American doesn't realize he has become captured and enslaved through excessive taxation and by the very dragon his forefathers had escaped from some two hundred years prior. The Bible says,

> "Who is able to make war with [the beast]?" (Revelation 13:4)

America began as a nation with a recognition of God and the Bible as a powerful influence on its foundation, the United States Constitution. The erosion of that foundation and the seizure of this once great and free nation has taken place gradually without the detection and knowledge of the populace.

# Chapter Twenty-Five

## Anglo-Americanism

A Global World Government in the modern era should not be viewed as a nineteenth century idea. The powerful forces of the Illuminati that unleashed the French Revolution in 1789 clearly show that a New World Global Order has been in the making since the eighteenth century.[1]

Throughout the 1800s in the United States, the idea of globalism was maintained by forces within the British Empire. Three prominent men in the latter part of the century who kept the dream moving forward were John Ruskin, Cecil Rhodes, and Alfred Milner.

Their desire was to unite the English-speaking people of the world, and to create a global commonwealth of nations patterned after the ideals of the British Empire, but controlled by English-speaking people of the aristocracy for the good of the world.[2]

## The Round Table-Ruskin, Rhodes, and Milner

John Ruskin, mentor of both Cecil Rhodes and Alfred Milner (father of the Round Table), was an ardent student of Plato's Republic, the same well from which Karl Marx drank.

Ruskin believed that the state should take control of the means of all production and distribution and organize them for the good of the people. "My continual aim has been to show the eternal superiority of some men to others, sometimes even of one man to all others." Ruskin taught that the ruling class of England had a world mission.[3]

## The World Mission

Ruskin taught the students of Oxford University that they were the next leaders of the mission. They were the ones who would carry on the tradition, the possessors of a magnificent tradition of education, rule of law, beauty, freedom, decency, and self-discipline.

He taught them that this tradition could not be saved unless it was extended to the lower classes of England and to the non-English masses of the world. If these two classes were not reached, the upper-class Englishmen would ultimately be submerged by these majorities, and the tradition would be lost.[4]

## Cecil Rhodes

Cecil Rhodes was one student in attendance in those days, and he caught the vision. As a result, with support from Lord Rothschild, he launched a lifetime of concerted efforts to federate the world.[5] His ambitious goals included:

- The extension of the British rule throughout the world;
- Perfecting a plan of emigration from the United Kingdom for colonization by British subjects of all lands where the means of livelihood are attainable by

energy, labor, and enterprise;

- The ultimate recovery of the United States of America as an integral part of the British Empire;
- The consolidation of the whole Empire;
- A system of colonial representation in the Imperial
- Parliament which may tend to weld together the disjointed members of the Empire;
- The foundation of so great a power as to hereafter render wars impossible and promote the best interests of humanity.

All this he endeavored to do without mention of material reward, an idea fashioned after the religious brotherhood of the Jesuits, "a church for the extension of the British Empire."[6]

The ideas of these men, advanced by the backing of Anglo-American banking houses, created secret societies, which in turn made secret agreements between England and the United States.

These secret treaties brought the two countries together into an Anglo-American alliance with the secret goal of a New World Global Order. In England, the secret society, which operated in London, was called the Round Table.[7]

When the planned seizure of the United States economy finally occurred in 1913, the formation of the two-horned beast (the world capital conglomerate) was complete. The conquest of mammon (money) enabled the concentration of financial power in the hands of an elite. What they needed now was a new world political system to manage the aspirations of the British dreamers.

The first attempt at a New World Order was the League of Nations. It came at the culmination of World War I. The general idea of the League of Nations started during the war with a group of Allied statesmen, notably British and American.[8] Winston

Churchill supports this view.The League of Nations was an Anglo-Saxon conception arising from the moral earnestness of persons of similar temperament on both sides of the Atlantic.[9]

**The League Fails**

The League of Nations, which was put forward by Woodrow Wilson, failed to gain entire acceptance. Paradoxically, though the rest of the world accepted the idea of the League of Nations, factions within the United States resisted the plan. The plan to create a League of Nations failed.

**The Council on Foreign Relations**

Other powerful men who were disciples of Ruskin joined their lives and fortunes with Rhodes and later formed the Round Table. Alfred Milner became the chief trustee after Rhodes' death. Round Table groups were established in other protectorates and the United States. In 1919 through 1927, the U.S. group became known as the Council on Foreign Relations, or the CFR.[10]

The story of how the secret society of Rhodes/Milner axis extended its influence to the United States is supplied by Dr. Carroll Quigley:

The American branch of this organization, called at times the Eastern Establishment, has played a very significant role in the history of the United States. Since 1925, there have been substantial contributions from wealthy individuals and from foundations, and firms associated with the International Banking Fraternity, especially the Carnegie United Kingdom Trust, and other organizations associated with J. P. Morgan, the Rockefeller and Whitney families, and the associates of Lazard Brothers and of Morgan, Grenfell, & Company.[11]

The CFR today has over two thousand members who represent the elite in government, labor, business, finance, communications and the academy. The primary reason the CFR remains virtually unknown to the American people is because of Article II of the CFR bylaws. This article requires that the meetings of the membership remain secret, and anyone releasing the contents of these meetings is subject to instant dismissal.[12]

The intellectuals who founded the CFR felt there was a need for a world government but that the American people were not ready for it. After the League of Nations treaty failed to pass the Senate, the CFR was founded specifically to condition the people to accept a world government as being a desirable solution to the world's problems.[13]

Many of the founders had been involved in the negotiations leading to the Treaty of Versailles after World War I, including:

- Colonel Edward House (who was secretly involved in the selection of Woodrow Wilson and operated behind the scenes as a secret secretary of state);
- Walter Lippmann (later to become one of the liberal establishment's favorite syndicated columnists);
- John Foster Dulles (later to become President Eisenhower's secretary of state);
- Allen Dulles (later to become the director of the Central Intelligence Agency);
- Christian Herter (later to become Dulles' successor as secretary of state) were deeply involved with the formation of the CFR. [14]

**Financiers of the CFR**

The original money behind the CFR came from J.P. Morgan, John D. Rockefeller, Bernard Baruch, Paul Warburg, Otto Kahn, and Jacob Schiff, among others. Two of those named above were present at Jekyll Island for the drafting of the Federal Reserve

Act. Two of the most outstanding names were J.P. Morgan and Paul Warburg, who (through Kuhn, Loeb & Co.) represented the Rothschilds of England.[15]

On November 25, 1959, in an issue of its own publication, Foreign Affairs, Study No. 7, the CFR detailed its own exact purpose:

Advocating the building of a new international order which may be responsible to world aspirations for peace, and for social and economic change; an international order including states labeling themselves as socialist (Communist). The words "new international order" are catchwords for a New World Global Government.[16]

**The Testimony of an Insider**

This is what former Rear Admiral Chester Ward (U.S. Navy, ret.), who was a member of the CFR, told the American people about the intention of the CFR.

"The power clique in these elitist groups have one objective in common; they want to bring about the surrender of the sovereignty and the national independence of the United States. A second clique of international members in the CFR comprise the Wall Street International Bankers, and their key agents. They want the world banking monopoly from whatever power ends up in control of global government. They would probably prefer that this be an all powerful United Nations Organization, but they are also prepared to deal with a One World Government controlled by the Soviet Communists if the U.S. sovereignty is ever surrendered to them."[17]

Ward went on to say that their overall influence is used

in promoting disarmament, subverting U.S. sovereignty, and suppressing national independence into an all-powerful One World Government.

Membership in the CFR reads like a veritable "who's who" in American politics. Forty-seven members of the American delegation to the founding of the UN were CFR members. At least twelve of the last eighteen secretaries of the treasury were CFR members. The Department of Defense, created in 1947, has had fifteen secretaries, nine of which have been CFR members.

Every Allied commander in Europe and every U.S. ambassador to NATO has been a member of the CFR.[18] Since the inception of the CFR, almost every U.S. president has been a member. Although Ronald Reagan was not, his key appointees were.[19]

The CFR and the Round Table form the hidden governments of the United States and Great Britain. They have been forged together for the purpose of bringing about the dream of Ruskin and Rhodes: a New World Global Order.[20]

# Chapter Twenty-Six

## The Two-horned Beast

It should be no secret at this point that the two horns of the second Beast are the two supposed and alleged Christian nations, Great Britain and the United States of America. These two nations—through secret Anglo-American agreements which began in the late 1800s—were brought together and are moving the whole world into a Global World Government, or New World Order.[1] It is the function of the two-horned Beast dubbed the False Prophet to serve the interests of the Beast system.

> "And he.causeth the earth and them which dwell therein to worship the first beast" (Revelation 13:12)

Here is the clear scriptural evidence that this second Beast, the False Prophet, works to construct the last phase of the first Beast.

These two horns, or kingdoms, were taken over by the international money powers seated in London.

The world community views both the United States and England as Christian nations, but the truth is that underneath this appearance there is a hidden government. Today, it is referred to as the deep state.

> "He had two horns like a lamb, and he spake as a dragon" (Rev. 13:11)

The inability to see this as fulfillment of biblical prophecy is due to the lack of a clear perception of European and American history.

In addition, we get no help from Western theologians that remain in darkness, blinded by the dualism of their dispensational theology and a naïveté that arises from a "Yankee Doodle" gospel.

It is a sad fact that America has become an instrument in political wrangling in the hands of the "god of this world." The failure to perceive this truth perpetuates the descent into darkness. The Bankers Money Machine

**The Bankers Money Machine**

It is through the creation of "wars and rumors of wars" (Matthew 24:6) that the internationalists have been able to create the condition that warrants a global socialistic state. They have flooded the world with red ink and have brought economic bondage through debt and usury, thereby enslaving the people of the world. How do wars and rumors of wars create debt and usury?

When the Federal Reserve Bank was created in 1913, it effectively mobilized the credit of the United States of America. This meant that the Fed, along with the European banking system, had the necessary resources to lend to the nations on new and unprecedented levels. Now, with this new tool in hand (the labor force of the United States guaranteeing loans to the world), the internationalists could swamp the world in debt.

How? By creating wars so that nations would borrow to build their war machinery. It takes billions to build great warships, planes, and weapons for warfare. Imagine the bank that would underwrite loans to the nations energized for war.

This is exactly the motivation that empowered the global planners: the creation of war just to make tremendous sums off interest from loans to the nations. One could even back both sides since the outcome made no difference and interest income would be made from both sides.

Then, after the wars end, nations would have to rebuild their infrastructure, loans would be made again to rebuild the houses, the factories, the businesses. Over time, this money making strategy could produce absolute economic power over the entire earth.

Isn't it an interesting coincidence that World War I began in 1914, immediately after the internationalists established control of the American banking system (the Federal Reserve) and the mobilization of American credit? The beginning of the hostilities that plunged the whole world into war are unclear to this day. Could it have been the international bankers that started the war to end all wars?

Through intrigue, through stealth, through manipulation of the nations, this has been the plan of the international banker elite: seizure of the earth through the creation of enormous debt. The magnitude of the global debt is staggering. The United States has been completely seized and enslaved. The national debt of the United States is greater than the total debt of the entire world.[2]

## The Cold War

In the Western world (especially North America), the apparent collapse of communism in Eastern Europe has been lauded as democracy's greatest triumph, a tribute to the success of the free enterprise system. What has not been perceived, however, is that communism has produced the first stages of a global socialism.

It has come about by communism serving as a counterweight to capitalism. The Cold War between the East and West created huge military expenditures for both sides to maintain the balance of power. The need for both parties to maintain military equilibrium created the necessity for enormous amounts of capital.

The bankers stood ready to loan. Once again, the use of the bankers' insidious printing press—and their ability to foment wars and rumors of wars—has further mired the world in debt. Thus, the bankers greatly advanced their economic grasp and control of the planet.

Since communism has been a chief ingredient for the bankers' scheme in this decade, let's back up and trace its roots.

## Communism

The notion of communism as British invention is not a new idea. The articulation of communism was put forward by Karl Marx, whose mentor was British industrialist, Frederick Engels. The primary reason for the expounding of this politico-economic ideology was to thwart the spread of democracy to Europe, which was advancing and succeeding in the United States.

The foundational principles of nation building expressed in the Monroe Doctrine, based upon George Washington's advice of avoiding entanglements with Europe, had to be countered.

These principles were beginning to be imported into Germany, and they posed a tremendous threat to British economic supremacy. The Industrial Revolution that came to the British Isles brought astounding revenues into the coffers of the Bank of England and the Empire itself.[3]

The controllers of Britain were fearful of potential competition on the world scene. They didn't want the rest of the world to industrialize and compete with British goods and markets. Thus came the Communist Manifesto and Das Kapital, whose fundamentals at the time espoused international free trade which, of course, was a contradiction to the Monroe Doctrine's ideology of protectionism.

Internationalism was a tremendous advantage for the British since they already had control of world markets, and it was a terrible disadvantage to the rest of the world whose economies were already exploited by the British. Communism was invented by British subjects, but its basic elements were taken from Illuminism. The basic strategy of communism was to stage economic war with continental Europe and the United States. The objective was to rule and maintain control of world markets. The actual roots of communism go back to Adam Weishaupt.[4]

### The New World Order in the Twentieth 20th Century

Later in the twentieth century, when the idea of globalism had matured, the front for the breakout of the New Global World Order was exported to Russia in the Bolshevik Revolution.[5] The czar would not borrow from the Western banks, which would have enslaved Russia through debt and usury. He had to be overthrown.

The ideology of world communism (having been established

through the internationalist-financed Bolshevik Revolution of 1917) established the necessary counterbalance: communism weighted against democracy/capitalism. Since World War II, the two have melded into an emerging global socialistic state.

The initial funding for the revolution came from a Rothschild-controlled banking house in the United States called Kuhn Loeb & Co.[6] The leadership and intelligence of the movement was supplied by various Marxists who lived in New York. Some were Jews who had become atheists and repudiated their ancient Hebraic ancestry. Many were not Jews, but all, like Karl Marx, had a fanatical political zeal to build a nation state that would encompass the whole world, a global Masonry.

Although the primitive breakout of this ideology can be traced to the French Revolution in 1789, the Bolshevik Revolution further advanced what has yet to come: a "World Government which seems destined to be seated in Jerusalem."[7]

After the Revolution, the Russian state struggled to keep on its feet, and had it not been for the propping up of the Russian economy by the West, there would have been total failure of that regime during the '20s and '30s.

When World War II was coming to an end, the Allies allowed the war to drag on unnecessarily, thus giving an opportunity to the Russians to seize Eastern Europe. A window of truth that supports this allegation can be seen in General Patton's march through Italy, which was mysteriously rerouted through France. Why was he not allowed to invade Germany and end the war? He was willing, ready, and able to take his troops into Berlin.

This military faux pas has never been understood by the world, but the truth is that the Russians needed time to come down into Eastern Europe. The bankers needed their antithesis. The politicians followed orders. General Patton was too good at being a soldier and military man; he was messing up the predetermined plan of the plotting bankers.

These strategic political decisions were made to enable communism to serve as the great antithesis to capitalism. This would lead the way for the inevitable synthesis of capitalism and communism into global socialism, which has now begun to emerge worldwide.

The successful effect of the antithesis (USSR) upon the West, when one lives in the West, is difficult to discern. The international mega-corporations owned by the international elite have created the tyranny of centralized capital and the increasing disappearance of the American entrepreneur. Freedom is being lost quickly, and the ability to compete against the enormity of centralized capital is almost impossible. The tremendous debt created by the necessary military defense of America from the antithesis (Russia) has enslaved the West.

**The Coming Trouble**

In the Middle East another plot was unfolding, and the banker's fingerprints were all over it. Earlier in the century, the British Round Table, under the leadership of Lord Balfour, determined to make the land of Palestine a Jewish homeland. Principally involved in this decision-making were the Rothschilds, the principal owners of the Bank of England.The British mandate came to be known as the Balfour Declaration, but the Jewish banking house of Rothschild was in the middle of the mix.

Even though the Rothschilds had abandoned their biblical Judaism, they maintain—as do all Jews—a genetically patriotic sense of loyalty to the land of the patriarchs. After the homeland for the Jews was set up in 1917, the Rothschilds were involved in extensive purchases, literally buying back the land from the Arabs.

Today, the land contains some six million Jews, thanks to the political and economic efforts of the Rothschild. But is this current return of the Jews that which the ancient prophets long ago predicted?

While it took the Balfour Declaration, two world wars, and the Holocaust to set up the state of Israel, it is not the final fulfillment of biblical prophecy as most Christians believe. The shocking fact of the matter is that through extensive writings by contemporary Christian writers, Christians falsely have been led to believe that this is the case. But it is clear that the theocratic state of Israel will not be set up by man—not even the contrivances of powerful and deceitful bankers of Jewish origin.

> "And it shall come to pass in that day, that the Lord shall set his hand again the second time to recover the remnant of his people…and shall assemble the outcasts of Israel, and gather together the dispersed of Judah from the four corners of the earth."(Isaiah 11:11,12)

This particular scripture is often cited by Christians as the fulfillment of prophecies for the Jews' current return to Zion. But under close scrutiny, this promised second return of God's people to the land already had occurred when they, His people, returned from Babylon. The first return being when they returned from Egypt by the hand of Moses.

But there will be a a significant gathering when the world will be transformed and the whole of even the animal kingdom is dramatically changed. Scripture, if read in context, shows:

> "The wolf also shall dwell with the lamb, and the

> leopard shall he down with the kid; and the calf and the young lion and fading together; and a little child shall lead them. And the cow and the bear shall feed; their young ones shall lie down together: and the lion shall eat straw like the ox. And the sucking child shall put his hand on the hole of the asp, and the weaned child shall put his hand on the cockatrice's den." (Isaiah 11:6-8)

**The Real New Age**

The time period in which this peculiar occurrence takes place has not yet come. These curious traits of animal behavior are unique and have never occurred. Nevertheless, they distinctively bookmark the exact nature of that time of return. The time period comes when the whole world is renewed by God during the millennial reign of Jesus Christ on earth.

It is during the millennial reign that the curse upon the earth is lifted and these remarkable and unprecedented changes in the animal kingdom occur. When that day comes, then God will signal for a worldwide return of the Jews to Israel. They will all come home—all, not just a portion. There are over seventeen million Jews living in the world today. They will all live in safety in the Promised Land of Israel. This is hardly the case today, as Jews live in constant fear and dread of their Muslim neighbors.

Since, according to biblical prophecy, the return of these people is yet in the future, then what has the world been witnessing from the beginning of the twentieth century in the Zionist movement, the Balfour Declaration, and the birth of the state of Israel in 1948?

**The Great Snare**

The answer to this question is both deep and prophetic.

What we are witnessing in the Middle East and Israel today is the setup of the great snare. David said,

> "Let their table become a snare before them: and that which should have been for their welfare, let it become a trap." ( Psalm 69:22).

Jesus also explained that this trap is one that will come over all the earth.

> "And take heed to yourselves, lest at any time your hearts be overcharged with surfeiting, and drunkenness, and cares of this life, and so that day come upon you unawares. For as a snare shall it come on all them that dwell on the face of the whole earth." (Luke 21:34,35)

The events that are taking place today are all leading to the fulfillment of Scriptures.

These events are the snare to the Jews and a trap to the whole world.

# Chapter Twenty-Seven

## Islam's Crescent Moon

The land of Israel is often called Palestine. The Jews prefer Israel of course, and the Arab Muslims prefer Palestine. It always irks me when Christians refer to this land as Palestine because it demonstrates a glaring ignorance of history.

When Abraham of old lived in the fertile crescent, he was promised by God that he would have a son who would become heir to the promised land. But after many years, his wife Sarai bore him no son.

Abraham grew weary of waiting on God to give him a son, so he decided to have a child by his concubine, Hagar; she was an Egyptian girl. Hagar conceived and bore him a son whom he named Ishmael. At the time Abraham, was called Abram but it was prophesied that this son Ishmael would be a "wild ass" of a man and his hand would be against his brothers. And so it has been through history even to this day.

Then God reminded Abram that He would indeed fulfill His promise, and a year later Isaac was born through his real wife Sarai. The Jews became descendants of Isaac and the Arab Muslims the descendants of Ishmael.

Consequently, Hagar and her son Ishmael were banished and sent off because of the conflict that arose between Sarai and Hagar. She and her son Ishmael moved eastward to the area known as the fertile crescent.

Yet, it was because Ishmael considered himself the first born of Abraham, that he was entitled to the land grant which came to be known as the "Promised Land."

Nevertheless, he never stopped believing he was the rightful heir to the Land of Promise. This attitude and the attending hostility he passed on to his descendants. After all, he felt cheated and betrayed. At least, that is how he reasoned.

To this day, the hatred lives on in his progeny. The Jews are the tragic historic recipients of the terrible ancient hatred from their Arab Muslim half-brothers.

Since that time, from around 2000 BC, to this very present day, the controversy rages between Arab Muslim and Jew. In the book of Revelation chapter 12, there is depicted a dragon with seven heads and ten horns. This is, of course a reference to Satan and his plan for global dominance, but out of the dragon's mouth there flows a torrent of water.

> "Then from his mouth the serpent spewed water like a river, to overtake the woman and sweep her away with the torrent." (Rev 12:15)

There has been an unrelenting filth of hatred pouring out upon the Jews for thousands of years. Is this not the river of filth coming forth from the mouth of the dragon? The most apparent today is the vile coming forth from the Muslim world on the Jews and now toward the Christians as well.

Regardless of the world's conceptions, or who the land belongs to, God deeded the land to the descendants of Isaac. Yet the controversy rages to this day. In the mind of the Arab Muslim world the land to whom it belongs remains unsettled.

The land of Israel has indeed become a snare in that it is totally surrounded by nearly two billion hostile Muslim

Arabs who want nothing more than to drive the rightful descendants of Isaac into the sea.

**The Kaaba**

When Ishmael moved eastward, the influence of the Kaaba wafted up from the area of Saudi Arabia. The Kaaba was a shrine that provided a fixed place for the worship of some three hundred and sixty gods.

Several hundreds of years even before the setup of the Kaaba, coming from the land of Egypt, there was a mortal, who invented the lunar calendar. He was also known for inventing weights and measurements, and he had a vast knowledge of the stars including knowledge of the procession of the equinox. He was also known for the invention of writing as well as numerous other facets of knowledge. He was head and shoulders above all of the people of his time. The man was a genius. While his actual identity is up for academic discussion, he was most probably the man Enoch of the Bible.

After he left the earth his renown continued, and he became known as Thoth or the "Moon god."

One can visit any papyrus shop in Cairo, Egypt and view the immortal image of Thoth, the "Moon god." There he can be seen as a man with the head of an Ibis bird standing in front of a scale. Thoth is seen taking notes as to the results of the weighing.

The scale bears a feather on one side and a human heart on

the other. The idea is that if the feather outweighed the heart, then it was the sign of a good man as he was being weighed in the balance. On the other hand if the heart outweighed the feather, then the heart of that individual was full of sin and the person would condemned to the underworld.

As the world turned toward darkness, this man Thoth became deified and he was considered to be a god. Again, he was termed to be the "Moon god" due to his invention of the lunar calendar.

An interesting aside, Thoth was also known to be a messenger to all the gods. Hundreds of years later, his renown spread to Greece. In Greece, he became known as Hermes the messenger god. Grecian culture private labeled Thoth to the name Hermes. When the Grecian empire was divided up amongst the four generals of Alexander the Great, the general Ptolemy Lagides, went to Egypt to establish a shrine for Hermes. The area became know as Hermopolis. It was of course a tribute to Thoth.

This "Moon god" idolatry was taken down to the Kaaba the land whose influence would overtake Ishmael and the "Moon god" became the greatest god of the three hundred and sixty gods of the Kaaba. His name to them was Al Elah, the greatest god. The name Al Elah has morphed into Allah. "Allah Akbar," as the name is shouted out, means the greatest god.

Today, he is represented as a crescent moon on the thirteen flags of the Muslim nations and also on top of every mosque, but the derivation of the "Moon god" came from Egypt and the deification and paganization of the great man into a god derived its beginning from that part of the world, the land of the pyramids; Thoth was his Egyptian name.

Moon god worship was an enormous contradiction to the

worship of Yahweh, and so it is to this day. The conflict has raged for over four thousand years. Jeremiah the prophet described the enmity between the moon god and Yahweh as the "ancient hatred." And so it is.

When the Jews left Egypt and wandered for forty years in the desert, they crossed the Jordan and came into the land of promise; it was called Canaan. But their crossing of the River Jordan is very instructive and noteworthy. It points to another massive preference by God between the Muslim "Moon god" and the Jews' Yahweh.

The Jews crossed over the Jordan at Jericho. Jericho was a fortified city, but it was also known as the city of the "Moon god." The Jews were commanded to circle the city for seven days and on the seventh day the city walls fell down by supernatural forces.

This was God/Yahweh's commentary on how He felt about the "Moon god," called Al Elah, and on whose side He stood. But the Jews later fell under the spell and influence of the "Moon god" and as a result Yahweh destroyed their temple twice and then He also destroyed their city.

The Jews after the two destructions of their temple were subsequently cast into the wilderness of the Gentiles for two thousand years.

Islam, today, is the child of the "Moon god" of yesteryear. The malignant religion has spread throughout the world, and even America has tragically fallen under its spell and is on the same track as the Jews had thousands of years ago. The Moon god, no doubt, was and is a powerful religious force in the world.

**The Jews Table**

Now that millions of Jews have returned to the land of

God's promise to Abraham, and with such hostilities surrounding, them, their table (the land) has become a snare. Especially as Muslim Iran, the region's leading sponsor of terrorism with nuclear weapons looming, stands ready and eager to destroy the land of Israel. It will be interesting to watch how Yahweh protects his covenant people from the age- old river of hatred from the people of the Moon god.

We can with certainty know what ultimately happens. The end of the matter is predicted in the 12th chapter of the book of Revelation.

In the end, we have an image of the woman who is clearly identified as Israel. She is identified in that she brings forth the male child who is Jesus. There, she is surrounded by twelve stars which represent the twelve tribes of Israel. She is cloaked with the sun. But in the image in Revelation 12, she is standing on the Moon.

The fact that she stands on the Moon shows the ultimate victory of Yahweh and the woman, Israel over Islam.

# Chapter Twenty-Eight

## Fire from Heaven

"And he doeth great wonders, so that he maketh fire come down from heaven on the earth in the sight of men." (Revelation 13:13)

When nine and twelve year old Orville and Wilbur went out to play, little did they realize that their playful antics would lead to discoveries that would revolutionize and transform the world, and drastically alter the way men think about time and space.

Orville and Wilbur Wright stumbled onto the hidden mysteries of flight. Dreams that men had dreamed for thousands of years were realized by the discoveries of these two unusual boys. The hidden wisdom of flight was revealed to the inquiring minds of the two brothers. The mastery of the heavens, which belongs to the birds alone, was now to be given to mankind.

In those days, provincial minds reasoned, "If the heavens belong to the Lord, then man has no business in the sky. After all, if God had intended man to fly, He would have given him wings like a bird." Today, as we look back on that line of reasoning, we laugh, but the horrific applications that came as result of the Wright brothers' discoveries make one wonder if those old-timers didn't have a point to be made.

If man's incredible intelligence were to be taken away, how could it be said that he is made in the image of God? The real issue, then, is not so much what is known about the principles of the universe, but rather what is done with that knowledge. This is a matter of conscience.

The problem, of course, is that, collectively, man's record on his trek across the annals of time is very poor when it comes to the use of knowledge. In the last one hundred years the world has dramatically progressed technologically, but at the same time there has been a corresponding decline in morality.

Has technology created a better human race? Morally, the answer is decidedly no. While man has become more sophisticated, his nature remains the same. But this is not an indictment on technology. The peculiar nature of the human race appears to be that what is meant for good man seems to turn into evil. Unless he has a remarkable conscience alteration, we all tread on a slippery slope.

**The Knowledge of Flight**

When the knowledge of flight arrived around the turn of the nineteenth century, it was not considered by the masses to be of any great significance. People did not really believe much would come from it. Yet within a few short years, flight began to play an extremely important role in the First World War. Man had invaded the realm of birds, and now new possibilities lay before him. He had risen above the terrestrial environment and placed himself in the seat of the heavens. Flight!

It had taken thousands of years to arrive, but the unconquerable had been conquered. What was next, the Moon? People scoffed. Flimsy little airplanes (Jennys) that were made of balsa wood and cloth could hardly be taken seriously. But eventually more and more was learned. Soon airplanes were able to cross the Atlantic Ocean. A voyage that took months by boat could now be made in a day. The world was made smaller by one man full of courage and bravery.

The momentous transatlantic flight by Charles Lindbergh immortalized flight and made it the most exciting scientific breakthrough of its day. Both Europe and America were startled by the significance of this marvelous and heroic deed. Lindbergh was swarmed by crowds and parades as the world marveled at the magnitude of the magnificent accomplishment.

The skies today are traversed with ease as powerful jet aircraft transport millions of around the earth. Today, Lindbergh's flight seems so small in fact even trivial, but it was that flight which caused a quantum leap in men's minds concerning the possibilities of flight. One of those possibilities was the utilization of flight for war.

**Nations Will Rise Against Nations**

The imposing of one nation's will over another's took on tempting new possibilities with the new technology. The vision of a Global Empire came under greater consideration in the mind of Adolf Hitler. Soon airplanes were armed with bombs. The world was at war. The airplane that was once made of cloth and balsa was now made of lightweight metals and able to lift great cargoes of weapons.

London and Poland were bombed by Hitler's Luftwaffe in his blitzkrieg warfare. In return, Germany was bombed by an armada of B17s. Cities were literally incinerated by fire storms. Tens of thousands of people died—not just by the explosions of the bombs, but by the resultant intense fire that sucked up all the breathable air.

America discovered how to make nuclear weapons. During the war with Japan in the Pacific, nuclear bombs were dropped on Hiroshima and Nagasaki. The intense fires from the blasts created temperatures as great as the sun. The cities were totally destroyed, incinerated by fire. People were burned beyond recognition. Many of those who survived carried the awful scars both in their memories and on their bodies from the fire that came down.

Later, Vietnam experienced the finest technological advancement in fire storms. Massive air raids brought down unimaginable devastation on the country's villages and forests. Napalm bombs wiped out mile after mile and village after village.

Then in the Gulf Wars with Iraq, the awesome air supremacy of the Western nations brought great fear in the nations of the world. What an object lesson was served to the peoples of the earth. Who would dare go to war with the world's ultimate police force? Fire would come down.

Especially now, enormous and incomprehensible strides have been made with laser-guided bombs and rockets. Not to mention drones particle beams, lasers, and exotic weapons that we have not presently caught wind of. What fear! But the ultimate has yet to come in the seizures of the utmost high ground.

**The Ultimate High Ground**

While military strategists rethink the necessity of airplanes (due to the tremendous success of guided missile technology), others have revised their thinking concerning Star Wars, or the Strategic Defense Initiative. While uncertainty reigns over the development of this technology, most probably it has been black boxed and is being secretly funded.

The Star Wars technology initiated by President Reagan is a laser technology, the brainchild of the Reagan administration. It is the absolute safest defense against incoming missile weaponry. As of this writing, that systems conception was almost thirty years ago. What has become of it after almost three decades? Is there a space-based laser technology?

When it is finished, if it's not already, the reality of it being turned over to the United Nations may be unlikely, but whoever controls that system will militarily control the world, for they will have the finest technological ability to call "fire down from heaven."

Finally, there is the UFO phenomena. While this subject lies beyond the credible grasp of the sensibilities of the average person, recently hundreds of testimonies from very credible men suggest that something is up.

One of the more perplexing stories that throws credence into the realm of potentially prophetic fulfillment occurred several years ago. According to high ranking military personnel, an American spacecraft that was headed toward the moon with a nuclear device was disabled by several beams of light from a UFO. It was destroyed, unable to finish its mission. The military believed it to be a plasma beam that disabled the spacecraft.

These men also testified that the United States has recovered crashed UFOs, and have been able, through their research, to implement technology recovered from the alien spacecraft. Considering the track record of the human race and the nature of man, this is not good news.

Remember these signs are accomplished by the False Prophet.

> "And he doeth great wonders, so that he maketh fire come down from heaven on the earth in the sight of men." (Revelation 13:13)

# Chapter Twenty-Nine

## The Image of the Beast

The agent of Antichrist is, of course, the second Beast of Revelation thirteen, the False Prophet. Who he is has already been revealed. He is dubbed the agent of Antichrist because he is the one who fleshes out a kingdom for the Antichrist at the end of the age. The kingdom of the Antichrist is a Global World Government that the Bible calls the Beast. It was shown in the previous chapter what the ultimate policing power is for this dark Utopia, but to control the world there must also be a vast communication system and mind control network. Everyone must be programmed to march to the same drum beat. There must be a universal focal point. There must also be a universal economic system, as shall be pointed out in the following chapter.

What is to be disclosed in this chapter is the second tool, or miraculous signs that the False Prophet uses to deceive the nations of the world into accepting the Global World Government.

"And [he] deceiveth them that dwell on the earth by

> the means of those miracles which he had power to do in the sight of the beast; saying to them that dwell on the earth, that they should make an image to the beast, which had the wound by a sword, and did live. And he had power to give life unto the image of the beast, that the image of the beast should both speak, and cause that as many as would not worship the image of the beast should be killed." (Revelation 13:14-15)

In Revelation 13:14, the "image of the Beast" contextually comes into the picture after the healing of a fatal wound to one of the imperial heads of the Beast. Since the various heads of John's first Beast (seven heads in number) have been assigned (Egypt, Assyria, Babylon, Persia, Greece, Rome, and the British Empire), the revived head will be that which comes out of the seven, or seventh.

> "And the beast that was, and is not, even he is the eighth, and is of the seven, and goeth into perdition." (Revelation 17:11)

The visible emergence of the eighth head is clearly the United Nations. It was established out of the fallen (slain) British Empire, empowered by the funding and support of America and domiciled in New York City on Manhattan Island. Its initial inception was sourced in the League of Nations, which failed. President Wilson's League of Nations, with its Fourteen Points, was the invention of the British Round Table—which in the second decade of the twentieth century sought to establish the Ruskin-Rhodes Milner dream.

When the League failed, it was renamed the United Nations and set up following World War II. At its core we find British fingerprints, but it was the combined effort of England and the United States that set it up.

The image of the Beast, according to Scripture, occurs after the healing of the fatal head wound to the Beast and the resurrection of the Beast's seventh head into an eighth head. In light of Scripture and history, was it possible that the image of the Beast could have been present in the later part of the 1940s, at the termination of World War II?

It is the function of the False Prophet to set up the image of the Beast. Since the False Prophet has been identified as England and the United States (represented by the two horns), the fact that the entity is present in the 1940s assumes that his signs or powers were also present. What is the image?

**What is the Image?**

The Greek word that is used to explain the second attesting miracle of powers of the False Prophet is not the word idol but the word eikon.[1] In the ancient world, an idol was usually a figure that was hand-crafted out of wood or metal. Often it was made in the likeness of an animal or bird. The idol of Moloch, for example, had the head of a bull and the hands of a man. Many times, idols were replications of demonic powers, and people would actually bow down and worship them.

Even the ancient Jews fell into this problem and were chastised by God when Aaron made a golden calf that the people bowed down to worship. When Moses, went up to Mt. Sinai to receive the Ten Commandments, and came back down, he ran smack dab into this revelry of idol worship and went ballistic. As a result, God smote the people with a curse and thousands died.

But that is not the word that is used to explain the image of the Beast. The word that explains the image is the word eikon. Whereas an idol is more a vis-a-vis representation of an image, eikon is better rendered "likeness." Here is an analogy that helps our understanding.

The disciples came to Jesus and asked, "Should we pay taxes?" Jesus answered, "Give me a coin. Whose eikon [image] is that?" They said, "Caesar's." The point is that the coin was not an exact replication of Caesar—which is what an idol would be—but rather a likeness of Caesar's image (eikon) on a coin.

The False prophet makes an eikon, a likeness of the Beast, not an exact representation of the Beast. It is important to remember at this point that the Beast that John saw in symbolic form represented a system of successive empires stretching from the Egyptian Empire through time to the United Nations.

This brings up an important consideration. What would an eikon look like that was a likeness of a system—a geopolitical system that has existed for five thousand years? This is a most perplexing and mind boggling consideration!

**Nonetheless, the warning from the Law:**

> "Thou shalt have no other gods before me. Thou shalt not make unto thee any graven image [idol], or any likeness of anything that is in heaven above, or that is in the earth beneath, or that is in the water under the earth: Thou shalt not bow down thyself to them, nor serve them" (Exodus 20:3-5)

In the Law, God instructed his people concerning idols. Perhaps man's lack of attention to this one principle has set him up for the greatest deception the world has ever known.

The global worship of the Antichrist is the False Prophet's

objective. But what does the word worship mean? The idea of worship in biblical Greek is best understood as an act of submission, as though one were bending his knee and kissing the hand of a king seated on his throne. This is an accurate picture of worship. It means submission, adoration, reverence, or awe.[2]

In order to evoke this kind of worshipful response from the global masses, the False Prophet gives life—and the ability to speak—to the eikon (or icon) of the Beast.

There are two words that explain the word life in the Greek language. One is the word zoe, and the other is the word pneuma. The word zoe is the word from which zoology comes, and it means "animate life." Zoe is life that only God the creator can give. The word that is given to explain the life that the False Prophet gives is the word pneuma. This word pertains to spirit life or spiritual life. Spiritual life is given, but not zoological life.[3] Spirit is intelligence. In addition, it is clear that the icon that speaks, which has spiritual life, also appears after the fatal head wound of the first Beast has been healed. It is the second tool in the hand of the False Prophet, a tool he uses to enslave the whole world in a global worship.

Clearly, the last great global empire was the British Empire, which was slain and now has given way to the eighth head: the United Nations. This could only happen with the presence of the second Beast.

Scripture teaches that he is contemporary with the first Beast and that his function is to build the final form of the Antichrist's system. Through his tools, he builds the final facet of the Beast system. Since he must be on the scene, his tools must also be present; he uses the tools to build the New Global World Order. His tools are the great signs or attesting wonders.

But how do you give spiritual life to an icon which

represents a system (the Beast system) that is over five thousand years old? What is the icon likeness supposed to look like? The answer to this question is crucial because it is the tool (or power) the False Prophet uses to bring the whole world into submission and worship.

What is this image of the Beast, the second power of the agent of Antichrist?

**Television Technologies: The Image of the Beast**

Since World War II, television has reshaped the American psyche. In all areas—entertainment, politics, marketing, education, and the presentation of news—TV has become the foremost pervasive conveyor to our subconscious and pre-suppositional psychological grid. It has relocated and replaced the marketplace, the soap box, the pulpit, and the family.

On-line shopping, using the same technology as TV, has become a respected and accepted form of shopping. In addition, we have on-line banking. Whether we want to face it or not, television, laptops and smartphones, have retooled not only America but world thought and has shrunk the world into a global commune.

With the exception of the workplace, TV technologies are the dominant force in American life and the world. We are rapidly being assimilated by television into a global culture. Because of TV, the world has invaded our homes so that a man's home is no longer his castle or his retreat from the world. It is our marketplace, our political forum, our playground, our school, our theater, our recreation, and our link to an escape from reality. It is the vice which reflects and shapes our assumptions and a means of assaulting those assumptions. It cuts through every socioeconomic, geographic, and cultural group.

It is the single binding thread of this country and the world. It is the one experience that touches young and old, rich and poor, learned and illiterate. A country which was too big for homogeneity, filled by people from all over the globe without any set core of values, America never had a unifying bond. Now we do. Now it is possible to answer the question, what do Americans do? They watch TV.

And how much TV do they watch? The average American family watches the television screens for an astounding six to eight hours per day.[4] That means the average child is spending more time watching the image of the beast than he is going to school. In the 1980s, there were more than 150 million TV sets that were turned on for an average of seven hours a day. In the early part of this century it is possible, given the continued growth, that we will spend more hours watching the tubes than the hours given to sleeping.

We already know the average citizen spends one fourth of his waking hours in front of the television technologies.[5] The only activity that takes more of our children's time is sleeping. There is no question that TV and its various other modes holds unparalleled power over America— more than schools, parents, or churches.

George Gurban, dean of the Annenberg School of Communication of the University of Pennsylvania, put it this way:

"In only two decades from 1946 to 1966 of massive existence, television had transformed the political life of the nation, had changed the daily habits of our people, had molded the style of the generation made overnight. TV had made global phenomena out of local happenings; redirected the flow of information and values from traditional channels to centralized networks reaching into every home.[6]

In other words, television. and now laptops and phones have profoundly affected what we call the process of socialization, the process by which members of a species interact.

By its reach, the image has it is so pervasive that it can alter the American idiom overnight. Who can ever forget in the not too distant past the phrase, "Where's the beef?" when it swept the nation?

The tube has altered the eating and sleeping habits of most Americans. It has kept them up later at night, but it has also kept them home. It has broken the traditional patterns of how children learn. Television has altered the shape and speed of our knowledge of the world.

In the 1930s, even as national radio grew, the mass circulation magazines were a centerpiece of American life for learning the news of the world—and for escaping from it. But by the time network TV was just twenty-five years old, the dominant weekly magazines—such as Life, Corners, and Saturday Evening Post—had all died out. The most widely circulated magazine was TV Guide.

The sheer power and reach of the technology is one reason why we understand so little about it. Its swift conquest of America can be linked in large measure to the fact that TV, as an instrument, reflected one of the populace's most insistent desires: to be left alone. In 1946, there were 7,000 TV sets in America. In 1947, there were 178,000 sets, with an estimated audience of one million.[7] In 1948, Milton Berle began his run on NBC, which helped explode production to 975,000 TV sets. One year later, 3,000,000 sets were made. By late 1949, TV drew forty-one percent of the radio audience.

This new medium—by accident more than design—was in the hands of relatively few people. And less and less by accident, these few people found themselves relatively free from effective control and accountability. This system had grown and taken shape in large measure because the invention had created new categories of reality, new sources of power that the government could not even contemplate until they were firmly in place. By mid-century, TV had conquered America.[8]

In one sense, we had expected it all along; in another sense, we never knew what hit us."

## Chapter Thirty

# Television: Snow White's Poisoned Apple

Just how close are we to the return of Christ? How can we see the times and know for certain when that event will take place? Jesus himself reminded us that we were to watch and pray. He warned that with regard to His Second Coming, we were not to fall asleep. Sleep, of course, is characterized by simply being unconscious.

Today, not only is the world unconscious of the impending return of Christ, but so is the church. The world's unconsciousness is best explained by the scripture where people are saying,

> "Where is the promise of his coming? for since the fathers fell asleep, all things continue as they were from the beginning of the creation."(2 Peter 3:4)

The church, on the other hand, is like the famous story of Snow White. She was offered the poisoned apple, she took a bite, and she fell into a death-like sleep.

It can be said that in our time, we have no prophet to show us our signs. The enemy has laid siege to the temple. The poisoned apple that people have bitten into is television technologies, and the poison continues to spread a deadening sleep. Now we have hundreds of channels laptops and phones to watch. We can order movies brought directly into our homes and small phone TVs. Broadband expands the use of the computer to new levels of fixation and new records of wasted time.

**The Common Plague of Smut**

Major networks continue to loosen their standards to regain those who have strayed. But the overall move of the Telecommunication industry is the continuous slide into the bottomless pit of debauchery. If the moral slide of television wasn't enough, the avalanche of smut on the Internet is almost incomprehensible.

Pornography accounts for more than eighty percent of the downloaded material coming into our homes. With the onslaught of pornography injected into the viewing public, especially teenagers, we are indeed engulfed in perilous times.

In the final hours before his execution, Ted Bundy, the most infamous of all serial murderers, spoke of the influence of pornography in his life and its subsequent effect on his behavior. He attributed his serial killing to the powerful influence of pornography. If his self-analysis is true, then we can expect an enormous wave of violence upon women and children in the very near future.

**What is Morality?**

Morality is simply the standard that operates on the human conscience to monitor thought. God placed His ten spiritual laws within the human conscience. These laws were clearly defined to the Jews when Moses received them from God on Mount Sinai thirty-five hundred years ago. The ten spiritual laws were known to the Jews as the Ten Commandments.

These laws reflect God's divine nature, and because these laws were placed within man, he is a moral agent. But morality cannot completely control behavior. It is a restraining force, but we are left to choose. In this sense, mankind is created in the image of Elohim but sadly imprisoned in a human body of sin.

When man deviates from these laws (that is, when he transgresses them), and does not seek repentance and forgiveness, his conscience darkens, he loses sight of his identity, and he becomes even less than the animals. Animals are amoral. Mankind, the moral agent, in his transgressions from the law, failure without repentance becomes immoral.

Since every man is a transgressor of his conscience, he is caught in a trap. His failure to act in the way he knows to be in his conscience creates guilt. The conscience of man monitors good and evil, both externally and internally. That is, it was designed by God to screen thoughts that enter the mind through environmental effects, and it also monitors the personal thoughts that arise from within the psyche.

When the conscience is operating in a healthy capacity, it will reject immoral thoughts that are in conflict with the laws of God, which are written on the inner conscience. Thus, morality functions in direct relationship with human conscience.

The human conscience, to be perfectly clear, is like the door to a castle: once it is broken down, the castle can be invaded and overcome. Pornography is an attack on the moral conscience.

Morality, based on the God-given law inscribed on the human conscience, was verified to the Jews on stone tablets. These laws clearly express God's standard of righteousness and form the basis of human morality. In the Western world, this concept is expressed as the Judeo-Christian ethic.

The human conscience stands to defend the inner person (or the subconscious) from the attack on morality. As human beings grow, they are either reinforced in their conscience, thus defending their inner person, or they are inundated and eroded by the opposite forces, which mitigate against this principle. This was the fate of Bundy, who became the serial killer.

Since the world defines the inner person as the subconscious mind, it is hard to make a point as to what the spiritual implications are in this context. Most people, including Christians, accept the notion that whatever isn't conscious mind is subconscious mind.

They mistakenly accept the world's definition as true. The fact of the matter is, what men call the subconscious mind is actually a man's spirit. The attack upon morality is an attack on the door to a man's spirit. If the door (conscience) is broken in, the man's inner temple (his spirit) is assailed and— as in Ted Bundy's case—possessed.

Since we are spirit encased in a flesh body, the attack on our spirit is an attack on who we are. It is an assault on our personal identity. Ted Bundy is a classic example of the war that rages over a man's temple. Bundy became the antithesis of what God intended for him to be.

**How the Image of the Beast Works**

Television has been seized by forces that long ago began, on a massive scale, to break down the foundation of Western Civilization. The Judeo-Christian ethic must, in the eyes of the world planners, be overthrown in order to create a One World Global Government. The stakes are high as more and more people bite into the forbidden fruit of television and the its various outlets called the media, slide into smut.

To bring this into focus, it must be seen that if there is to be a final hour of organized lawlessness, it must begin with a total breakdown of God-defined morality—so that men might be conformed to a global empire.

Since the founding fathers of this great nation developed the Constitution based on a Judeo-Christian ethic, this country, only to a degree, remains an obstacle in the plans for a New World Order. If ever one wanted to make a case for an external restraining force beyond the inner conscience of an individual, America would be a good topic of conversation.

Is there any wonder why the current President, Donald Trump, who seeks to defy the global trend towards a one world government, is encountering tremendous headwinds. And where is the hurricane forces coming from? They are coming principally from the hijacked media.

Take America out of the world as a Christian nation and restraining force watch what happens. But this is exactly what TV, the Internet, film industry and social media have done to this country. They are all part of the image of the Beast. The Judeo-Christian morality is sinking fast. Destroying Christianity is exactly what the New Global World Order is about.

**The New World Order Morality**

This empire will not be based on laws of conscience placed by God.

Television and the entire media has insinuated itself quickly into the global psychological fabric of man's subconscious. It is the major tool being used to reshape the world away from the Judeo-Christian ethic and into a new international standard, a standard that is not based on God's original intent for judging thought or behavior. It could be said that the basic spirit of TV, and media in general with fewer and fewer exceptions, is antichrist.

This media assault on the human conscience through the display of sexual immorality and the effect of that morality has seeped its way into the political fabric of both the United States and western Europe as well. If we are honest with ourselves, the grim reality of the False Prophet's great miraculous powers are indeed working wonders as he invisibly goes about transforming the globe into a one world government. And nowhere is this more evident in the application of the media on society.

This particular section has dealt with TV and its derivative, computer monitors (which are the same technology). This technology is clearly an instrument in the hands of the global planners.

And it's not just television. The image of the Beast is any reflection of the mores, folkways, and values of the outside world delivered through TV and TV technologies.

It exists in all media outlets from the internet, to radio, to smart phones, to Hollywood, or any kind of broad net that is cast over the general world wide population. Print media is also part of the mix.

The image of the beast is a mind numbing mind controlling development of the beast system that totally and mentally intoxicates mankind. It is the power of the media.

The image of the Beast is the media, and all the world bows to it, and worships it.

# Chapter Thirty-One

## Here Is Wisdom

> "And that no man might buy or sell, save he that had the mark, or the name of the beast, or the number of his name."(Revelation 13:17)

Jesus had much to say about money and riches. In fact, throughout the scripture, many references speak of the power and transient nature of the riches of this world. Two examples are found in Proverbs.

> "Wilt thou set thine eyes upon that which is not? for riches certainly make themselves wings; they fly away as an eagle toward heaven."(Proverbs 23:5)

> "When thou sittest to eat with a ruler, consider diligentlywhat is before thee: And put a knife to thy throat, if thou be a man given to appetite." (Proverbs 23:1-2)

In other words, wealth can buy people. Money has the power to make men compromise their values.

**The Anti-christ will Master Money**

The coming world ruler, the Antichrist, will not only gain mastery over mammon (wealth), he also will be the consummate money manager when he ends up with all the gold, silver, costly stones, and treasures.

> "But in his estate shall he honour the God of forces: and a god whom his fathers knew not shall he honour with gold, and silver, and with precious stones, and pleasant things."(Daniel 11:38)

> "But he shall have power over the treasures of gold and of silver, and over all the precious things of Egypt." (Daniel 11:43)

While this scripture most likely is a reference to the historical Antiochus IV, the fourth of Syria, elements of prophecy tend to repeat over time. The Anti-christ will no doubt be a very power man.

When Jesus spoke on wealth, he used the phrase "mammon of unrighteousness." The word mammon in the ancient world meant "riches," akin to a Hebrew word meaning "to be firm, steadfast"; hence, mammon is that which is trusted.[1]

> "No man can serve two masters: for either he will hate the one, and love the other; or else he will hold to the one, and despise the other. Ye cannot serve God and mammon." (Matthew 6:24)

In other words, one is either serving God or money. He either puts his trust in one or the other.

During the temptations of Christ in the wilderness, the prince of this world, Satan, offered Jesus the kingdoms of the world and all their glory. There was a catch to the offer: Christ had to first bow down and worship him. Jesus passed on the overture, but someone will succumb (or already has succumbed) to that temptation and will take the devil up on it.

When that day finally comes, the means for world control will come through the concentration and accumulation of wealth or mammon. The god of this world is mammon, and he who controls mammon will control the world.

Since 2 Thessalonians 2:1-12 teaches that the coming of the day of the Lord will be preceded by the Antichrist, the forces pressing the world toward the New World Order will be noticed in the place where wealth or money is accumulating and concentrating. When the final and complete mastery of wealth is accomplished, the Antichrist will soon appear, and the failure of mammon will follow.

Scripture instructs the faithful to:

> "Make to yourselves friends of the mammon of unrighteousness; that, when it fails, they may receive you into everlasting habitations." (Luke 16:9)

When mammon fails, those who put their reliance in it will be enticed into a new economic system.

### The New Global Economic System

The new system, as predicted in Revelation, will no longer have any medium of exchange that man historically has been accustomed to using. What is coming is a total departure from anything man has ever known in the transacting of goods and services. There will be absolutely no exchange currencies such as dollars or coin or gold or silver. It is described in the book of Revelation as a system where only a mark is utilized.

> "And he causeth all, both small and great, rich and poor, free and bond, to receive a mark in their right hand, or in their foreheads: And that no man might buy or sell, save he that had the mark, or the name of the beast, or the number of his name." (Revelation 13:16-17)

Human nature is a strange thing. Usually, people do not make changes in their lives unless they are struck by a tragedy or a catastrophe of some sort. Since people naturally resist change, they will especially not favor changes in the way business is transacted today.

It is because of this human characteristic that the coming cashless system is gradually being foisted on the peoples of the world. Its coming is hardly being noticed. It is being phased in through electronic funds transfer and debit cards.

In order for its final form to be imposed, however, there will, in all probability, be a great depression or world banking collapse. The United States' debt continues to soar, as of this writing more than twenty trillion dollars. The population of the United States at this writing is 326 million people That does not include illegal immigrants.

Each citizen's share of that debt amounts, as of this writing, is hovering at seventy thousand dollars. The debt is not static; it has been growing at the rate of more than a billion dollars per day since September 28, 2001. This incredible debt explosion (along with the J.P. Morgan Chase Manhattan derivatives exposure) places the system ever closer to a massive collapse. When the economic system sputters and fails, the timing will be ripe for a cashless system.

**Justification for a Cashless System**

The Great Works of Cainism

There are in the world today a great many complicated and distressing problems that a cashless system would seemingly correct, thus making a cashless system seem justifiable and reasonable.

**Drugs**

The international drug cartel could not operate and would fold overnight. A cashless society, run by a mark on the hand or the forehead, would eliminate the world's greatest social problem.

If there were no cash, local and domestic growers of drugs would not be able to sell their goods.

Since drug money cannot be taxed, huge fortunes accumulate within the drug cartels, and the money barons (the Fed) cannot regulate it.

The people of the U.S. would do almost anything to stop the flow of drugs, due to their destructive effect on the youth.

The price tag to fight drugs through military expenditures would be cut to almost zero.

**Counterfeiting**

As technology progresses, almost any novice today with the right equipment can counterfeit currency. During WWII, millions and millions of bogus dollars were printed in Eastern Europe. This counterfeit currency flooded the market, causing great damage to our economic system. The destruction of a country's currency is a form of warfare. A mark that would eliminate cash would safeguard against the counterfeit currency problem.

**Credit Card Fraud-Identity Theft**

Credit card fraud, which now amounts to tens of billions each year, and the subsequent wrecking of people's credit through stolen cards would be totally eliminated. In addition, the elimination of identity theft will be solved by this innovative system.

**Illegal Immigration**

The uncontrolled influx of illegal immigration, which destabilizes economic systems, would totally stop. Remember, no one can buy or sell without a mark. And those coming into a country instantly could be tracked and found.

**Underground Economy**

In every nation, there is an underground economy that goes untaxed. Hundreds of billions of dollars flow through the underground economic system in the U.S. alone. The underground economy in other nations is the dominant system of those countries. How does a nation pay its debts without taxation? And how can a government tax income that cannot be tracked?

Underground economies, typified by merchants selling goods on street corners, are growing in South America, draining billions of dollars in taxes and other revenues from their financially troubled governments.

Even self-employed professionals such as doctors, dentists, lawyers, and psychologists are going underground. The underground network provides millions of jobs—and extra income for the otherwise unemployed, but experts say the gross national product of many countries would grow fifty percent or more if underground economies were counted.

In a recent newsletter distributed in Brazil, the First National Bank of Boston said that the informal economy "dodges direct taxation, but uses public schools and roads. It avoids massive paperwork, government inspection, and the burden of dealing with thirty-eight government entities to make simple business decisions." The bank estimated "an additional thirty, forty, or even fifty percent of extra economic activities are out there bubbling away and contributing to a much more sizable gross national product."

**Crime**

A cashless system would eliminate a great deal of crime where the motive was cash. Think of it! All kinds of crime eliminated as money becomes virtually impossible to steal. There would no longer be bank robberies, skimming of funds, diverting of money. Sophisticated white-collar crime would be no more. The economic system would be perfect. The justification for a cashless economy becomes very self-evident when we look at the deteriorating conditions of society. A cashless system would eliminate the sex trade industry.

**The Federal Debt**

If a man gets to far over his head in debt, he has to declare bankruptcy. When this happens, he has to start over again. After all, you can't get blood from a turnip. The same is true for a country.

The federal debt is so enormous that there is simply no way it can be paid back. Every year, the compounding interest and continued borrowing to finance the annual budget deficit worsens the problem. The new monetary system will eliminate the problem. It will streamline the system that simply doesn't work any longer.

The third world nations are already set for any kind of change that will bring them out of their hopelessness—especially nations like Brazil, Argentina, and Venezuela. The countries of Africa are buried under a mountain of debt and cannot meet the interest service, let alone pay off the debt. The United States, in its new spate of deficit spending, is back on the pathway of monumental debt and inevitable bankruptcy.

**Health Care**

One of the greatest social and political problems of the last several decades is the issue of health care. Although the United States has the greatest health care system in the world, millions of people in the United States are without affordable health care protection. When the taxation problem is solved (through the elimination of the underground economy), the amount of money to finance a universal health care program will immediately materialize. Universal health care will be available for anyone in the world by just taking the mark of the Beast. Imagine that! The mark will establish you as a world citizen.

**Global Peace**

The most appealing aspect of the mark will be a great reduction in the threat of war. Since many wars come from the love of money, eliminate money and what follows is the elimination of most wars and crimes. At least that is the promise. The people of the world will see this idea as the greatest boon to peace the world has even known. They will reason that the tradeoff, which is the total loss of privacy will be more than worth it. Anyone who doesn't go along with the idea will be viewed as a malcontent and rebellious, a war monger, an enemy of the state. How could anyone not want peace? The pressure to conform to the new economic system will be enormous.

The people today who live in the great cities literally fear for their lives. The streets are unsafe. Assaults, rape, and murder are the order of the day and the night.

Try wearing the colors of the local street gangs and see what happens. The people of the great cities are ripe for any reasonable answer. The people of Earth are weary of conflict and poverty. All that is needed is a round of massive inflation and the new system will flow in on the cries of the people. The new world economic system will make the world safer.

### Protection and Prevention of Terrorism

The mark of the Beast will eliminate terrorism. The war on terrorism will ultimately be waged by eliminating cash. The men who destroyed the World Trade Center were able to function because they used cash. If every man, woman, and child had to be marked with an electronic number, the whole of society could be tracked. This would be an enormous selling point. The world will finally be safe from terrorism.

### Y2K set the Stage

After the Y2K bug failed to work its woe, very few people realized the terrible potential for world calamity. More than two hundred billion dollars was spent to correct what could have been history's worst disaster. Those that grasped the terrible danger worked feverishly to rectify the problem. As a result of the colossal effort to fix the problem, the world's electronic interconnectedness was greatly enhanced.

The IRS boasts that before Y2K there were sixteen mainframe computers that managed our entire tax system. Today, as a result of Y2K, there is only one. That is control! All it will take is global fiat currency system failure and the nations will be in position for total cashless, international electronic money: the mark of the Beast. The stage is set. All the currencies of the world are fiat. Every currency is being inflated. They are all set on a crash course towards worthlessness. It is just a matter of time.

**A World Banking Collapse**

Is it really possible that there could be a world banking collapse? Today, all the world's banks are fashioned after the Bank of England. They all function fundamentally the same with what is called "fiat" currency. A fiat currency is a currency that is not backed by gold or silver; they exist by the fiat (or command) of the king. Bankers love fiat currency because contrary to gold which cannot be printed or manipulated, a currency can simply be printed. All you need is ink, paper, and a printing press. In other words, it can be inflated. Gold and silver on the other hand must be mined.

An enormous amount of human labor is involved in extracting the precious metals from the earth. Bankers hate gold and silver for this reason. They cannot alter it; they cannot inflate it. It is what it is: real money. Since the Clinton administration, the Federal Reserve has inflated the money (cash) supply over seventy percent. Alan Greenspan created seventy percent more cash flow by simply turning on the printing presses. The numbers for the FED under the chairman, Ben Bernanke, was more difficult to know, since the M-3 money supply was no longer made public. Since the Obama years, the Federal debt has more than doubled.

As a result, enormous volumes of cash entered the stock market as people took advantage of low interest rates and placed their bets on the stock market. The stock market exploded upward, forming a bubble.

Those who took the exhilarating ride will nervously watch as their paper wealth will begin to slowly evaporate. Unfortunately, they will also be taking the ride down. But the amazing thing is that the perception of the value of the dollar tends to remain by and large the same. How can this be?

The value of gold and silver has been manipulated by the bankers to maintain the perception of a stable currency. Gold and silver, even though they no longer are redeemable by currency, still function as a de facto standard of value of a currency. Why? Precious metals represent real money, or real value.

If the true measure of money can be manipulated, then the perception of inflation on a currency (the bankers' printing press) goes unnoticed. The bankers can continue to print money, which makes currency worth less, but the public never catches on to what is happening to the money in their pockets.

How do they manage to manipulate the price of gold and silver? Derivatives. They sell derivatives. A derivative is a contract that derives its value from something tangible—in this case, a gold or silver contract. A gold or silver futures contract is paper gold and silver. It is a promise to deliver an order of gold or silver in the future.

Let's say Kodak needs a million ounces of silver a year (Kodak uses enormous amounts of silver for film). They want to lock in a price today, but will take delivery in one year. If silver goes up in price, they made a smart decision because they locked in the price and saved money. Had they waited to buy later, it would have cost them more. This is a futures contract. They pay today's price but take delivery in the future.

The advantage for Kodak is they only have to pay a small

percentage to control those million ounces of silver until delivery is made a year later. Then they pay the balance. However, the risk is that even if the price of silver goes down, Kodak still has to pay the price they agreed to in the original deal.

These derivatives are used to control the price of the gold and silver commodities. How? By selling enormous amounts of paper gold and silver contracts, they flood the market and drive the price of those commodities down. The paper price effectively drives down the hard gold and silver price.

The gold and silver commodities have been rigged and manipulated for years. The big banking houses of J.P. Morgan/ Chase, Citibank, Goldman Sachs, and others are involved in concert with the Fed to manipulate the perception of the value of our currency by controlling the price of gold and silver. It is not a free market. But their ability to deceive the public is coming to an end. Either the fraud will be exposed, or the law of supply and demand will bring the truth out into the light of day. J.P. Morgan/ Chase has over twenty-four trillion dollar derivative exposure. They have sold far more gold and silver than exists.

What will come is a failure of the money system as we know it. Then the solution will be the Mark of the Beast and a cashless system, as predicted in Revelation thirteen.

## Chapter Thirty-Two

# Laser Scanning for Supermarket Automation

> "Here is wisdom. Let him that hath understanding count the number of the beast: for it is the number of a man; and his number is six hundred threescore and six."
>
> (Revelation 13:18)

When the universal product code (UPC) was invented and introduced in 1973 by IBM (a Rockefeller-owned corporation), there were five variations of the code, classed as A, B, C, D, and E. The A and E versions are most commonly used in grocery applications.

Its primary purpose at the time was simply daily inventory control. This eliminated the need for grocery stores to go through the tedium of counting what was left on the shelves after each day's business. One could merely take stock by punching in the request to the computer which calculated the day's business.[1]

**The Universal Product Code**

There are three major features of the UPC symbol:

1. The encodation uses varying width intervals of bars and spaces. This eliminates sensitivity to ink spread and allows the symbol to be read by scan lines not perpendicular to the bars.[2]

width intervals

0 1 6 0 0 0 6 6 2 1 0 4

**Fig. 1** UPC symbol showing width intervals for bar codes

2. The symbol can be read as two halves by the laser scanner beam and then combined in the computer system to yield the full 12-digit code.

0 1 6 0 0 0 6 6 2 1 0 4

Product ID Number

Manufacturer ID Number

**Fig 2** Two halves of UPC symbol

3. Laser Scanning Systems for Supermarket Automation

0 16000 66210 4

Guard Bar | Product ID Number | Center Bar | Mfr ID Number | Guard Bar

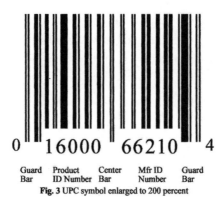

**Fig. 3** UPC symbol enlarged to 200 percent

4. The size of the UPC symbol may be as large as two hundred percent of the normal size, or as small as eighty percent of the normal.

Figures 1, 2, and 3 illustrate a standard UPC symbol, which is the machine-readable representation of the UPC code. A standard symbol consists of parallel light and dark bars of varying widths accompanied by numeric characters printed below each data character. The numeric characters are not readable to the computer; it only reads the barcodes. The numeric characters are for human consumption and represent the data which are encoded with the bars.

The left side of the symbol begins with a white margin and the guard bars (see Fig. 3) followed by the encoded number system character. This character is usually identified with a human-readable character immediately outside the left margin. The system character is followed by five characters. These characters represent the number of each particular product. Then in the middle are the center bars, or the center band, which are followed by five more characters representing the manufacturer number. The five data characters are followed by the guard bars and then the white margin.[5]

It is very critical to focus on the understanding that the computer does not recognize numbers as we know them. The computers, with incredible speed, calculate the binary values of 1's and zero's contained in the width of the lines of the bars.

The data bars of the UPC carry specific coded information on the product identification information (the left side of UPC) and the manufacturer identification information (the right side of UPC).

The guard bars are, however, different in function than the data bars. The guard bars actually operate the computer. They are computer programming characters. They actually tell the computer when to start and stop picking up the data information.[4]

Of vital importance is the binary value of the guard bars. In Figure 4, on the right side of the UPC, the first data character next to the center bar is the data character with the equivalent numeric value of six. If you look at the design of that character, you will see it is exactly the same width as the guard bars.[5]

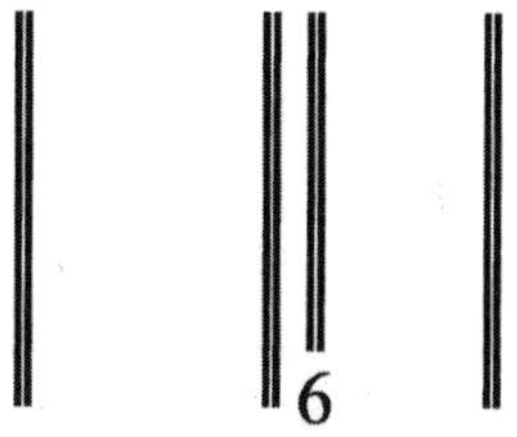


**Fig. 4 UPC width design of guard bars**

This pattern—light line, space, light line—conforms exactly to the dimensions of the guard bars. Remember, the computer does not know numeric values, only binary values. So, when the electronic scanner goes over the marks on each package as you check out from the grocery store, it is only seeing 1's and zero's. This is also true of the guard bars. The computer is seeing the guard bars in the language of 1's and zero's.[6]

Laser Scanning Systems for Supermarket Automation

**The Numeric Value of the UPC Guard Bars 666**

The most amazing thing is that although the guard bars encoded with three and five modules as 101 and 01010, they operate on the same root as the data character six, which is configured with seven modules. The three bars within the UPC that operate the computer are all in binary 101 and 01010, or the equivalent of the number of the data character six (see Fig. 5).[7] Though the encodings are different, the visible modules of 101 are the same.

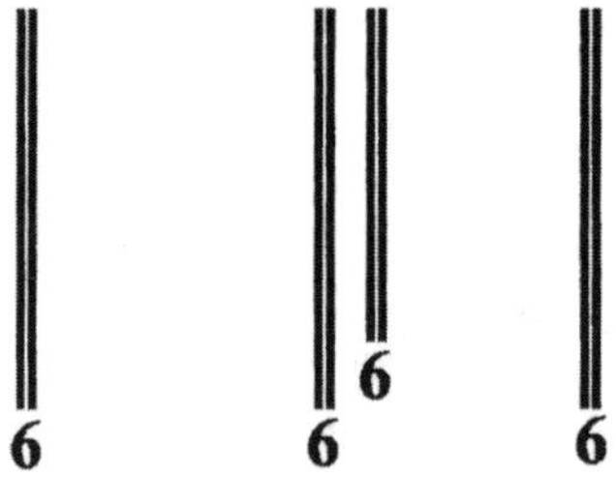


**Fig. 5 Binary value of guard bars**

The Universal Product Code is a mark run by three sixes. It was designed as a boon to control and keep track of inventory for businesses. When the time is ripe—due to the many global problems and the burgeoning world population—the mark will be applied to everyone for total world monetary control.

> "And he causeth all, both small and great, rich and poor, free and bond, to receive a mark in their right hand, or in their foreheads: And that no man might buy or sell, save he that had the mark, or the name of the beast, or the number of his name. Here is wisdom. Let him that hath understanding count the number of the beast: for it is the number of a man; and his number is six hundred threescore and six." ( Revelation 13:16-18)

**The Application of 666**

Here is a plausible scenario for how easily this technology can be adapted for a New World Order economic system. Everyone could be given the three programming characters (see Fig. 6).The Numeric Value of the UPC Guard Bars 666

These characters have been referred to as the guard bars and the center bar of the UPC. Each has a binary value of 101, which equates to the numeric value of six. Ostensibly, each person could be given the three computer programming characters 666. The technology can also be encoded in a chip.

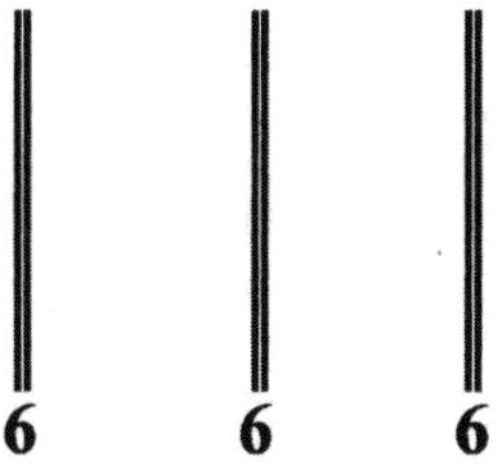


**Fig. 6 The three UPC sixes**

Each person could have three sixes which access the computer, and specific information concerning who they are and where they live (see Fig. 7). Then each could be given an electronic banking number.

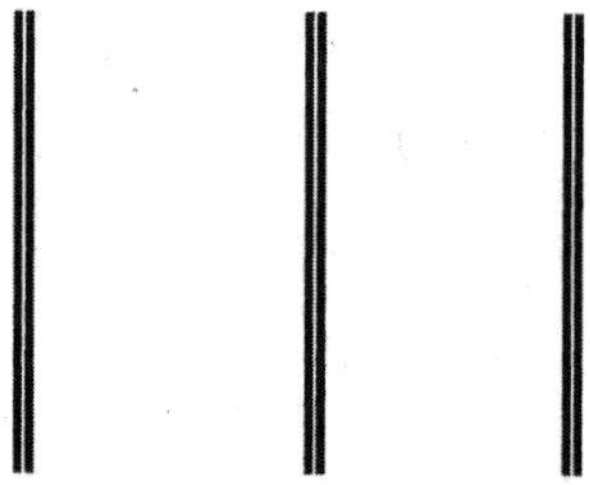

**Fig. 7 Preliminary framework for ID number**

## Laser Scanning Systems for Supermarket Automation

As can be seen above, the three sixes could serve as the computer programming characters. Then, as shown in Figure 8, the beginning bar codes of data are entered on the left side of the UPC. The data that have been added are 110 and 619.

The number 110 is the corporate ID number of the United States, and 619 is the telephone area code of San Diego. Every nation has a corporate identification number, which indicates the national corporate computer system containing the individual's location (in this example, the United States).The 619 number answers to a local area computer. So we have 61106196. Plausibly, 619 could reference a local computer.

110619

**Fig. 8 Data for personal residence**

The right side of the UPC could have the PIN (personal identification number). Every child born in the United States is given a Social Security number at birth. The PIN, no doubt, will be linked to that ID number. Since each area code computer system can contain up to 999,999 names, it can be seen that almost one billion names can be stored in the 110 (United States) corporate numbers system. We have added a six digit modified Social Security number that, hypothetically, could answer to the San Diego area computer district.

Once the mark is filled in, we have a completed PIN that allows the individual to do away with all earlier forms of identification. The sixes used to operate the computer by the laser scanner are the universal computer access number.

110619 266210

**Fig. 9 Completed personal ID number**

With this new system, an individual can travel the world without having to carry a passport, driver's license, credit card, or money. No money?

When a purchase is to be made say, the supermarket, the laser scanner could simply scan the merchandise. Then, with a handheld scanner, the cashier could scan the customer's hand or forehead (the mark will be on the hand or the forehead) and retrieve the necessary personal information for an electronic funds transfer from that person's electronic banking account. The electronic banking account will be linked directly to the individual's personal information on the right side of the UPC. With incredible speed, the EFT (electronic funds transfer) will deduct the amount of the purchase from the individual's electronic account and transfer the funds into the account of the store where the purchase has been made.

Electronic funds transfer technology has now been installed in gasoline stations, restaurants, supermarkets, and every kind of retail agency. Years ago in southern California, a prominent fast food chain initiated the idea using a company called Interlink. The system links certain local banks together in a banking network and allowed a bank card purchase for food at the restaurant. Now this practice is commonplace. The system automatically deducts the purchase price of the food from the individual's bank account and transfers the funds to the restaurant's bank account. This system of binary technology

Laser Scanning Systems for Supermarket Automation has been in place for many years as a forerunner of the coming 666 worldwide cashless system.

**Better than UPC Bar Codes**

There are a few limitations with the existing system. The

scanning laser needs a direct line of sight to the bar code, and the bar code itself needs to be reasonably clean and undamaged—one reason your cashier might have to swipe that bag of spuds four or five times before the scanner reads it.

Now there's something better—roughly six times better than bar codes. A very small electric crystal chip can be embedded into products to provide up to ninety-six bits of information. It comes from the Office of Naval Research.

The new radio frequency scanners can read the chip whether they have direct line of sight to it or not. The chips themselves are less than an inch long, with the antenna attached, and only about as thick as a pencil lead. The power source comes from the scanner. The new chips store enough information to uniquely tag just about every manufactured item.

The scanner reads not only the category and model number, but also a serial number for the particular item that bears the tag. The tags can be used for all kinds of marking, supply, tracking, inventory management, and logistical tasks. Checking out of the supermarket is as easy as pushing your cart through the supermarket's door.

As technology continues to advance, a cashless society is being phased in right before our eyes. The ultimate step will be when a mark is invisibly laser tattooed or a new chip is implanted on the hand or the forehead. There will be no fear of misplacement or theft of credit or debit cards. The mark's PIN number can never be forgotten since it is permanently on the flesh. When all the technology is in place and all the computers are linked, the mark will be usable worldwide.

Many will invariably ask the tempting question, "When will this all happen?" All it will take to bring about this new economic system is a banking failure. The J.P. Morgan derivative exposure, the massive fraud in corporate America, not to mention the printing of fiat money.

We are well on our way to a massive economic failure.

**The Red Sea of Worldwide Debt**

It is hard to understand the financial predicament of the United States. The national debt is more than ten trillion dollars. The yearly deficit seems to be running in excess of four hundred billion. The interest and the debt continue to accumulate at frightening speed. What this means is either tax increases or inflation.

There is no other solution to this ever-present crisis. Since both inflation and tax increases represent a greater burden on people, the system will eventually fall by its own weight of debt. The world follows the United States, so what is true for America is true for the rest of the world. When America entered the Great Depression in 1929, the whole world followed.

The global drug problem, domestic and Third World debt, terrorism, and strange cosmological problems are all creating the climate for a New Global World Economic System.

The idea of a debit system (as opposed to a credit system) has been here for many years. The American people, without a whimper, have been blindly accepting the phase-in. As the system is foisted upon America, some people are reluctant to pay their bills with electronic funds transfer, but they are powerless to fight the trend and the momentum the banking system is gaining.

**Radio Frequency Identification**

In the evolution of bar code technology, a new development is moving quickly to the forefront, which promises to answer society's greatest problems; Radio Frequency Identification.

Radio Frequency Identification or RFID is the latest

technological advancement that utilizes pulsating radio waves that are transmitted right from a bar code. What this advancement in technology means is that a new bar code has the capacity to send binary information through the air direct to a receiver, eliminating the need for scanners.

Presently, the technology allows information to be transmitted over distances of several hundred yards. But in the future, the emitting of bar code radio waves will no doubt span much greater distances.

As illegal immigrants fill our prison system, crush our health care systems, and destroy our economy, the cry from most Americans is reaching the ears of our politicians. In addition, the illegal immigration issue is complicated by the threat of terrorism. The answer to all these perplexing questions will no doubt be RFID.

In the past number of years, the UPC code has been miniaturized and inculcated into RFID chips. According to Wikipedia, Radio frequency identification (RFID) uses electromagnetic fields to automatically identify and track tags attached to objects. The tags contain electronically stored information. Passive tags collect energy from a nearby RFID reader interrogating radio waves. This is the new wave technology for the "Mark of the Beast."

An RFID system has readers and tags that communicate with each other by radio. RFID tags are so small and require so little power that they don't even need a battery to store information and exchange data with readers. This makes it easy and cheap to apply tags to all kinds of things that people would like to identify or track. How easily this technology could be adapted for use on humans.

The use of RFID is increasing rapidly with the capability

to "tag" any item with an inexpensive communications chip and then read that tag with a reader. Endless applications range from supply chain management to asset tracking to authentication of frequently counterfeited pharmaceuticals.

Applications are limited, in fact, only by the imagination of the user. That means, with imaginations running rampant, it's powerful way to instantly stop the world-wide Islamic invasion.

There would be no need for physical walls to defend porous borders. What an amazing solution to manage world peace. In fact, the scriptures say when the say the words "peace and safety," are used, "beware because then sudden destruction will come."

It has been forecast that the placement of the chip on humans will come shortly. Some have even indicated and projected it would be here before the year 2020. That remains to be seen, but the fact that the technology is here is without a doubt. In fact, there are a number of companies already producing them.

It will only take a massive crisis to bring it about. Most likely, a world economic collapse will precipitate the willingness for people to accept the chip so that they can go back to buying and selling. It will be the new money. The new technology is here and just waiting to be activated.

The long awaited mysterious Mark of the Beast is at hand.

**The Last Fullfillment**

The coming World Economic System will be just as the Bible predicted over two thousand years ago. It will be a cashless system run by a mark that will be placed on the hand or the forehead.

The mark will be mysteriously run by three sixes, and no one will be able to buy or sell except the one who has taken the mark.

Certain destruction will come upon all those who take the mark, for this is the ultimate economic system of the Antichrist and the Beast. Those who resist the mark are the ones who will live like vagabonds. These people will mainly consist of Christians and criminals who refuse to be involved in the system.

It seems logical to assume that since the United States leads the world that it, along with the western nations of Europe, will be the first to set into place the technology of the Mark of the Beast.

**Like a Freight Train**

These insights should make it clear that we are in the time of very grave spiritual danger. This third tool of the False Prophet, a revolutionary economic system, is being phased in, to bring about world economic control. A New World Order requires and demands a New World Economic System.

## Chapter Thirty-Three

# A Common Confusion

If the False Prophet is a system how can it be thrown into the lake of fire? This is a question that is frequently asked by those who have accepted the teaching that the False Prophet is a man. It is easy for the imagination to accept a man being thrown into a lake of fire, since he is an object. However, a system being thrown into the lake of fire is a problem for the human imagination because a system is not tangible.

The importance of the question is an enormous consideration. Let us use an analogy to explain. Have you ever flown in an airplane over the United States? If you have, you obviously noticed that you couldn't tell the difference between, say, California and Arizona. There are no lines separating the states like you would see on a map—and likewise across the whole country. There is only a continuous land mass.

That is because the United States is a political entity that in actuality, only exists on paper. If there were no state constitutions delineating and designating the borders and the boundary lines, there would only be a known land mass. That is exactly what we see from the airplane, the land mass. The United States only exists because men decided there would be a country with individual states. They drew up state constitutions and state boundary lines. The United States only exists on paper as a political entity.

Take the Constitution, the state constitutions, the IRS tax codes, and America's treaties and throw them into a fire. What do you have? The end to the political entity called the United States. Only the land mass is left—with, of course, houses, cars, people, etc., but no political or economic definitions remaining. America only exists, in a sense, in code. If you burn up the codes in a fire, you destroy the political reality.

The False Prophet is a symbol that represents a code, the outworking of which produces a political entity.

Before we press on, a computer code is a very strange configuration that derives its creation from keys on a keyboard. When a programmer writes within a code the outworking of that code emerges on a screen, it has absolutely no resemblance to the code itself. This is the same for the codes in Revelation. The symbols of Revelation are pictorial representations of spiritual codes.

In this case, the code of the two horned beast explains a political reality (America and England). If you throw the symbol (the False Prophet—the code) into the lake of fire (a spiritual fire), you destroy the code. When the code is destroyed, so is the political reality it has produced. The same thing happens if you destroy a computer code that has produced a program. Destroy the code and the program that it has produced vanishes. Ever throw an icon in the trash bin? No more program.

Apart from God, Satan is the master of code creation in the

spiritual dimension. Most likely, the tree of the knowledge of good and evil had to do with the invitation to the knowledge and mastery of code.

Consider the phenomena of movie-making. When we visit the cinema, we watch a movie on a screen which is the projection of light through a film strip. We hardly ever think of the film strip, but we could not see a movie unless there was light being projected through a cellulose film. All we know is that we are seeing an image on a screen.

The true essence of the movie, however, is not what we see on the big screen but the film strip itself. If one were to tear down the thirty-foot screen, it would not bring an end to the film strip. We could go to the movie house down the street and project the same film strip on that screen and—voila!—we could be back in business watching our movie. But take the film strip, throw it in a fire, and burn it up: That is the end of the movie forever.

The False Prophet (a code) is like the film strip that projects onto this world the code that it represents, a political system of the two kingdoms (England and the United States). Burn the False Prophet (the code) in fire (the lake of fire), and there is no longer the political system (England and the United States). The land mass still remains and is not destroyed- Only the political entity is destroyed.

Just like every beast in the Bible represents a kingdom (a political system), the False Prophet is also a political system of two kings, and he (or it) is destroyed.

One last note: Many have tried to say that since the word he is a personal pronoun, the False Prophet has to be a man. But in Daniel eight, notice that the two beasts identified as Mede-Persia and Greece are also characterized and presented with the personal pronoun he. Yet it is clearly speaking about two nation states represented by beasts. The pronoun he does not represent a man; it represents a symbol expressed as an animal. .

# Chapter Thirty-Four

## The Law

The two political constructs that have entered into the world, the Beast from the time of Nimrod until the present, and the False Prophet in the twentieth century are the manifestations of Revelation thirteen. Both have come into the world as a result of the failure of the "restraining force."It is stated in scripture this way.

> "For the mystery of iniquity doth already work: only he who now letteth will let, until he be taken out of the way." (2 Thes. 2:7)

The failure of the "restraining force" is because it is weak through the flesh.

"For what the law could not do, in that it was weak through the flesh, God sending his own Son in the likeness of sinful flesh, and for sin, condemned sin in the flesh."Romans 8:3. The Law is a fading glory. It was from the beginning of its introduction on Mt Sinai, and has been throughout time, But it was given as a tutor to bring us to Jesus, and the new covenant.

When God gave the Law (the Ten Commandments) to the Jews, He was placing before them the mirror of their inner man. The very Law of God is written on the hearts of men. Since God's laws are written within every man, the ten laws given to Moses were merely the reflection of man's inner conscience. What was the purpose? The giving of Law was intended to communicate the hopelessness of man's predicament and the utter impossibility to achieve the likeness of God. This revelation by God through the Law was both good and bad. It was good in that the laws declared God's own nature and that He was selecting a people for Himself and it was written written on stone. It was bad, however, in that it laid out a standard that was unattainable and virtually impossible to live by. It testified to God's righteousness but only proved that mankind was deficient and could live up to its lofty standard.

The Law was perfect because it was handed down by a perfect God. The Law expressed His righteous nature, but when imposed on the people, the Law had no power in and of itself to change the people to conform with His nature. It could not be lived out in humans.

The Law created a contrast and terrible conflict between the perfect morality of a righteous God and the imperfect and fallible man. No matter how hard a man tried, he could never live up to this Law. Thus, the Law, expressing the holy and righteous characteristics of God, was a curse to men..

The Jews, who were given the Law found themselves in an incredible dilemma of constantly dealing with the reality of sin—that is, the transgression of the Law due to the motions of sin in their bodies.

They were daily facing the terrible conflict, but the Law was given so they could come to grips with their earthly predicament. The giving of the Law was a wake up call. They had to ask themselves the question of how could these laws that rule the conscience—having been reinforced by the Ten Commandments on stone tablets— supply the answer to their dilemma? It couldn't!

On the one hand, the human conscience agrees with the Law given by Moses, but, on the other hand, man cannot perform the Law in his behavior or thought life. The Apostle Paul in his letter to the Corinthians called the Law the ministry of death.

Man is both like God, in that his conscience shows the work of the Law, and like the devil, in that he tends to live out in contradiction the very things he agrees are right and proper in his own conscience. This is why the Apostle Paul said, "woe is me."

**Mental Disease**

What does all this mean? The only solution for the predicament was to concede that man's conscience wasn't strong enough by itself to control a man's behavior. This paradox of conscience and a man's natural behavior (that daily functions in contradiction to his conscience) is the very source of most mental disease. The contradiction creates a huge identity crisis.

When God gave the Law (Ten Commandments) to the Jews, He purposefully gave an unlivable standard. Wasn't that cruel one may ask? Why did He do that? He did that to clearly point out that man's self-centered nature was estranged from God's nature. The contrast was necessary to pave the way for the only solution to the problem. It took over one thousand years to set the stage for the remedy..

The Law was given to break through to man and enable him to see his estrangement. God's nature and ways are not the ways of man. God's thoughts are much higher than a man's thoughts.

God's purpose was not only to show the contrast between God and man but also to show the impossibility of man ever getting out of the situation by himself. The Law was intended to communicate the hopelessness of man's predicament, and the utter impossibility of attaining to the likeness of God. Even by the sheer power of the human will with utmost attempt at obedience to His Law, it was still hopeless.

The Old Testament Law only made man more mindful of his moral inability and failure. The Law, as a covenant, could never bring one into perfection. Nevertheless, we are compelled to become perfect. The Law demands perfection, but provides no means. But how could God accomplish His desire to bring man to the point where he could perfectly fulfill and live up to the standard of the Law?

**The Temporary Solution**

Along with the Law, God instituted the temporary animal sacrificial system as a means for making up the problem for man's shortcomings. It was the principle of atonement, and again, it made amends and bridged the gap for man's inability to live up to the lofty standard of the Law.

Although the animal sacrificial system was rudimentary in its teaching mankind about justice, it was established to show that when a transgression of the Law occurred—either individually or corporately—there had to be a penalty assessed and a price paid for each particular transgression.

If a man committed murder, he was to die himself. If there was adultery, then a punishment for that sin was to be meted out.

But, in order to approach God after a transgression, there also had to be the spilling of the blood of animals. The animal sacrifices required a priesthood to administer the religious ordeal. The tribe of Levi was selected for this special responsibility.

It was, and is, the holiness of God that required the satisfaction for the transgression of the Law. Disobedience to the Law was, and is, depletion from the life of God. In order for man to be in right standing with God there had to be the remitting of sin. The expiation of sin is achieved through blood.

> "For it is the blood that maketh an atonement for the soul." (Leviticus 17:11)

The Law and the animal sacrificial system was instituted only to pave the way, and thus lead to a better and more perfect contract with God.

When the priests approached the outward temple, they took the blood of the animals and sprinkled the blood on various parts of the temple. The sprinkling of the blood by the priest spoke of the necessity for atonement in approaching God. There could be no approaching without the shedding of blood. There had to be a recognition of transgression(s) and the need for a cost. In this primitive system came the instruction and recognition that mankind was estranged from a transcendent God. In this way, the Law and the priesthood served as a schoolmaster that would prepare the way for an everlasting atonement.

And so it was, that because the atonement for sin was a continuous and yearly ordeal men were in remembrance of their transgressions. The conscience was perplexed continuously in a state of conflict with their behavior. This was and for many, even today, the horrific untenable situation for the human race.

Historically it was the Jews who were sovereignly selected

to be tasked and burdened with this knowledge. They were called to apply the rudimentary and imperfect atonement system in those days before Christ.

But the blood of animals utilized by the Jewish priesthood could not once and for all bring about a perfect atonement. And neither was their any power attached to the Law that supplied men with the empowering to live the Law. The Law merely declared the righteousness of God but there was no way men could live up to it. This is why in the book of Galatian it was called a curse.

But people who depend on following the Law to make them right are under a curse. As the Scriptures say,

> "They must do everything that is written in the Law. If they do not always obey, they are under a curse." (Galatians 3:10)

In fact rather than divine energy being supplied and given in association with the ability to live the Law it did the exact opposite. And because of this terrible consequence, the Law actually accentuating sin by energizing sin the Law was labeled by the Apostle Paul as a curse.

Here is why Paul said what he said what he said. From the Law it was written.

> "This is the blood of the covenant, which God has commanded you to keep. In the same way, he sprinkled with the blood both the tabernacle and everything used in its ceremonies." (Gal. 3:10)

In fact, the Law required that nearly everything be cleansed with blood, and without the shedding of blood there is no forgiveness.

The resolution for all is the one true antidote for the human condition.

## Chapter Thirty-five

# The Antidote

The collective consciousness of humanity has allowed the world to be inundated with evil. All the evil that enters into this world comes through the gateway of human beings. It is not just in our time, but throughout all time from "the garden" until now.

And the presence of the two beasts represents the collective effort through mankind in trying to fix the world trying to bring it back to Eden. But the sheer force of the collective human will is not the way. That way, is the way of self righteousness, and is the way of Cain.

Political constructs are the consumate and collective effort using law in a vain attempt to correct the world of all the evils that mankind has allowed entry into the world.

Today, the United Nations, is Cainism finest hour. And this is why the New World Order ( eighth head of the Beast) as it comes over the Earth, at the same time, we see the greatest outbreak of lawlessness.

> "For when we live according to the flesh, the sinful passions aroused by the Law were at work in bodies, bearing fruit for death." (Romans 7:5)

Not only is lawlessness accelerating amongst the masses it has become a glaring reality in the highest echelons of government.

**The Real and New Antidote**

The resolution is for all to come to the true antidote for the human condition.

> "But now, having died to what bound us, we have been released from the Law, so that we serve in the new way of the Spirit, and not in the old way of the written code." (Rom.7:6)

When Jesus died this is what happened. The Law crucified Christ, but while the Law was crucifying Christ, He was crucifying the Law.

Jesus brought in the perfect and everlasting atonement in Himself which totally replaced the Jewish sacrificial system.He wiped the slate clean for everyone of what the Law condemned, that is, for all who accept His atonement. Otherwise, it it is not applicable to those who chose not to accept what He accomplished by His atonement. For those who refuse to accept, they remain yet under the Law. Ultimately they face the judgement of the Law.

In totality, Jesus rescued a fallen race from it's colossal fall into the flesh, and by His rescue mission reactivated the empowering for the inner man. A man's spirit is his inner man and his true self.

Intrinsically, man does not need legal knowledge. Rather, he needs power to enable him to live above the motions of disobedience within his body.

While the old Law required the blood of animals to adjudicate for sin, God sent His Son Jesus, into this world as a more perfect sacrifice. Through His blood, man could finally have an everlasting, once and for all atonement. But the once and for all means a daily renewing.

In addition, the very life of God Himself, the Holy Spirit, is given to empower a person to escape the clutches of sin in the body. It is not as though sin leaves the body, though. The victory must be exercised daily, and occurs by the strengthening of the inner man ongoingly by the use of faith. It is by this "law of the spirit" a man or woman is strengthened in the inner man. This victory is called the mastery.

> "The law of the spirit sets us free from the Law of sin and death." (Romans 8:2)

**No Room for confusion**

Through proper understanding and response to the New Covenant, mankind can be free from mental disease, since most all mental disease is merely the result of suppressed guilt. (guilt is the feeling upon the conscience that occurs when one violates the Law) If proper response to the atonement through Christ's blood is not invoked, then guilt is shoved down through the door of the conscience into the human spirit (subconscious).

Mental disease is a legal problem with God that requires a payment against a violation of God's Law. The problem is complicated because in God's court, you are guilty when you violate the Law. But when an appeal is made to God on the grounds of the blood of Jesus Christ (the New Covenant and the daily sprinkling of blood), quickly there is an immediate release from guilt.

> “God has not given us a spirit of fear but of power and love and a sound mind.( I Timothy 1:7)

## Chapter Thirty-Six

# The King of the World

The final chapter in the conspiracy against God and man on Earth will be the coming Antichrist. Since the city of God was to be Jerusalem, the Antichrist will seek to set up the ancient throne of King David in Jerusalem. He will seek to establish himself as the king or the president of the world.

### Why the Throne of David?

The throne of King David has great eternal significance. Jerusalem, according to the ancient prophets, is to be the theocratic venue of Christ's millennial reign on earth. The forces of darkness will attempt to circumvent this plan. Through violence (followed by a false peace), the forces of darkness will set up the "man of lawlessness" (the Antichrist) in place of the rightful heir, Christ Jesus.

The Christian church's anxious longing for the return of Christ will continue until these malevolent events take place. Yet these events must take place before His earthly Kingdom can come. Millions of His people do not realize that when He returns, the kingdoms of this world will be finished and His Reign will last for one thousand years. In that reign He and those who overcome will rule with a rod of iron (Rev: 2:27).

Over the centuries, Satan—through his incredible strategy of the Global World Order—has been busily shaping the world for ultimate control. His desire is to once again seat himself in the place of the Most High this time on Earth. Isaiah describes the first attempt to usurp God's throne in the heavens. Satan will try again for God's throne on Earth. The throne of God on the Earth is the throne of King David (Isaiah 14:13).

When Christ walked on the earth, the original disciples expected an immediate restoration of the Davidic kingdom. They believed Jesus would immediately establish His rule (see Acts 1).

The disciples truly believed that Jesus was the Son of David, and that He would quickly move to restore the glory of David's Kingdom which had been lost for one thousand years (Matthew 9:27). Not only did Old Testament prophecy reveal Jesus as the coming Son of David, but when He arrived on the scene some two thousand years ago, Jesus clearly responded to that title.

Now, after more than two thousand years since Christ's day, the world is rapidly moving into a Global World System—both political and economic—that is, a counterfeit millennial kingdom. However, there is no apparent king (Antichrist) to run the show.

Yet, this entire false system should excite the hearts of every Christian; it is a major sign of Christ's return.

To sum up: Jesus is the Son of David who will come to rule the world. He will destroy this Global World System, which will have its initial locus in Western Europe and the United States but will eventually remove to Jerusalem. It will be ruled for a short time by the usurper, Antichrist, who will attempt to lay claim to the ancient throne of David.

**Who is the Antichrist?**

In the Old Testament, God used types as examples to foreshadow events that would occur in the latter years.

In the case of the usurper (who will come to take control of the Global World Government), there is an interesting Old Testament type. A careful study of this Old Testament type is important in that it may shed light in detecting the advance of the Antichrist.

**Old Testament Parallel is a Shadow and Type**

The parallel or shadow can be found in a story centered around King David at the time when his kingdom was firmly in hand. At that moment in Jewish history, Israel was a unified nation, not divided between north and south. It was at the height of its glory. But even though David's kingdom seemed firmly under control, his immediate family was having horrific problems.

The underlying reason for the internal discord came from problems that arose out of David's concept of marriage. King David was a polygamist. Even though David was a man who loved God and sought after Him more than any other in his day, his desire for many women led to tremendous problems within his own family. It seems strange that God never spoke to him on this matter, but allowed him to continue on in the grave error.

There came a time when a serious conflict arose among the children of his family. David had many sons and daughters from different wives. The problem arose with David's son, Amnon. He had an irresistible lust for David's daughter, Tamar (a daughter from a different mother than Amnon).

Amnon was sexually aroused by his half-sister so much so that he became emotionally and psychotically distraught. He sought counsel from David's nephew, Jonadab, a very shrewd man whom Amnon considered a friend. Jonadab counseled Amnon on how to manipulate Tamar into a compromising situation and then take her by force sexually.

Amnon took his advice, and Tamar was shamed. News of the rape came to Tamar's full-blooded brother Absalom, and as a result, Absalom deeply hated Amnon. Absalom waited for his father, the king, to deal with the debacle, yet David failed to act in a disciplinary way toward Amnon.

Absalom continued to hold to his hatred for Amnon. He reasoned that if his father would do nothing, then he would act independently (2 Samuel 13:24-39). After all, the Law of the Jews declared that:

> "And if a man shall take his sister, his father's daughter, or his mother's daughter… it is a wicked thing; and they shall be cut off in the sight of their people: he hath uncovered his sister's nakedness; he shall bear his iniquity." (Leviticus 20:17)

When the king delayed disciplinary action upon Amnon, Absalom took the Law into his own hands and made arrangements to murder his brother.

After he succeeded in killing Amnon, Absalom fled from Jerusalem and his father. He lived in obscurity for several years, but eventually he returned to Jerusalem to once again seek the favor of his father. David, however, shunned his son. Then Absalom, feeling justified and self-righteous about taking Amnon's life, conspired to usurp the throne of his father.

**The Usurpation of the Throne of David**

It is an interesting exercise to consider the machinations of Absalom's inner reasoning. Perhaps he felt that his father was too old and could no longer execute sound judgment. After all, didn't the Law require action against Amnon? Or maybe Absalom felt that, underneath it all, his father was really a weak man who couldn't act against his own family with the kind of punishment that the Law required for the crime of rape.

Whatever the reasoning and motivations, Absalom sought to usurp the Davidic throne. Absalom the murderer now became Absalom the thief and usurper. Satan himself is characterized in the New Testament as a liar, a thief, and a murderer. Absalom crossed a line in relationship to the Davidic throne and the holy city of Jerusalem and thus inherits the character of Satan. The Antichrist that is to come will have these same attributes; he will cross those same lines.

**Lucifer's Character**

Satan, as he is revealed in the Bible, was once an archangel. Lucifer's character has not changed; his modus operandi and his hatred toward God are still the same. He formerly desired to usurp God's throne. In Absalom we see the reenactment of that twisted character.

But not just any compromised human agent will do for the purposes of the "prince of the power of the air. "Just as the Body of Jesus was prepared by the Father to house the Spirit of Christ, the human body for the archangel spirit of Lucifer will most likely have to be specially designed for him as well. Only, the engineering for that body could likely be that of a scientifically cloned individual. With masterful computers and the science of gene splicing reaching its apex, the technology for that inevitable event is near at hand, or in the not too distant future.

But it does not have to necessarily be that far ranging and exotic. The Anti-christ spirit could come into any human vessel that is open to its access and has been genetically compromised. This can come from a mixed marriage and parents who are not of the same homogeneity.

Absalom's mother was Maacah, who was the daughter of Talmai. Talmai was king of Geshur. David and his men invaded the Geshurites. These were some remains of the Amorites and other ancient inhabitants of the country whom God for their inveterate and incorrigible wickedness, had commanded to be extirpated. Talmai may have had a recessive gene connection with Anak, who was a king of the giants. This may have surfaced later as a dominant genetic factor in Absalom.

The lineage of the Hamites is an interesting study. After the Noahic flood when all life was destroyed the giants reemerged. There were giants in the world before the flood, so how did they come back to when all life on the planet was destroyed?

They must have re-manifested after the flood a gene carried in someone's body genetics. There is evidence that Ham, one of Noah's sons had a wife with a connection in her family patriarchy to the giants. The Hamitic gene taint was carried along and was in Talmai. It was then in Maacah, daughter of Talmai and David's wife. King David unwittingly married into the gene pool of the giants

King David, in marrying Maacah, ventured outside the confines and boundaries of the Jewish instruction to only marry a Jew. Maacah must have been quite a beauty for David to ignore God's instructions. Hence there came a prototype Anti-christ usurper in Absolom.

## Implications of the Assault

When the Lord Jesus came to the earth initially, He had to fulfill every prophecy spoken of Him. Most specifically, however, He had to be a descendant of the royal line of succession of the kings of Israel. At the same time, He had to be born through immaculate conception by the Holy Spirit.

In other words, He had to be born of the seed of man and the seed of God at the same time. Hence, He would refer to Himself as the Son of Man and also the Son of God. Christ, however, could not have an earthly father; the blood of the human race was tainted with a curse. Life is transmitted by the blood, and the sin nature is passed on to each successive generation by the male side of the human race.

Christ, the incarnation of the living God, could not have the sin nature of the human race and still be God (Colossians 2:9). By being of the seed of the woman (through Mary) and yet being immaculately conceived (by the power of the Holy Spirit), God accomplished the task of not only fulfilling prophecy, but setting up the necessary ingredients for the rescue of the human race.

Mary was a descendent of King David through Nathan, David's son through Bathsheba, and therefore in the lineage of the royal King David. Through Mary's ancestry, Jesus obtained the titles of Son of Man and Son of David.

## Christ's Legal Inheritance

Jesus, however, would have had no legal claim to the earthly throne had it not been for Joseph. Joseph, His stepfather, was the key to the legal claim of Christ to the throne of King David. Joseph was a descendant of David too, only Joseph's line of ancestry proceeded from Solomon, from whom the royal line of the kings came.

Therefore, Christ's legal claim to the throne of David came

as a result of the marriage of Joseph to Mary before Jesus was born. This marriage was necessary to enable Christ Jesus to be the legal heir to the throne of David, even though Joseph was not the natural father of Jesus.

Furthermore, though Joseph could make the Lord Jesus the legal heir to the throne, Jesus could not be connected to the succession of the actual kings. His humanness had to come from Mary. This was due to another taint that was placed upon the kings at the time of King Jeconiah. This particular king was so evil that God had to literally take back a provision He had made. Jeconiah had transgressed to the degree that God could no longer keep His promise the original way He intended it. The legal rights could be conferred, but the literal seed would not descend.

**Of Jeconiah, God says:**

> "Write ye this man childless, a man that shall not prosper in his days: for no man of his seed shall prosper, sitting upon the throne of David, and ruling any more in Judah." (Jeremiah 22:30)

Joseph had to have a connection to the royal lineage of Solomon to whom God had made a promise that an heir would be forever seated on his throne. Joseph's genealogy, as it is traced in the book of Matthew, ends with his connection to the royal lineage of King David through Solomon.

One last important thing: Joseph had to be wed to Mary prior to the birth of Jesus to confer this legal right of succession. Had Joseph delayed becoming Mary's husband until after Jesus was born, Jesus would have been illegitimate. By wedding Mary before the birth, Joseph became the legal father of Jesus, imparting to Jesus the legal right to the throne of David (Matthew 1:24).

Had Absalom succeeded, had the conspiracy supplanted King David and his throne, it would have prevented Jesus from coming to the earth. It is conceivable that God could have worked out another virgin birth through some other party. However, that would have made Jesus Christ the Savior and not the coming King.

We see here the operation of the foreknowledge of God and the absolute literal fulfillment of prophecy. God, in His infinite knowledge and wisdom, worked out through time that His Son be not only Savior of the world, but also the heir to the throne of King David.

It must be remembered that Satan's murder of Christ at the hands of the Romans and the Jews was because Christ claimed to be King. Satan seeks a throne and a kingdom, as we have seen. When the throne of David was assailed during David's lifetime (by the adversary through human agency) and then again during Christ's lifetime, it becomes clear that this is Satan's purpose on the earth. He will try again, but this time by seating himself on the throne as a man of a One World Government.

## Lucifer's Clear Pattern

Lucifer, at one time, was very close to God. He was the anointed cherub. It was through an insurrection that the attempt on God's throne came. It was through an agent whom God trusted and who was given hallowed secrets of the government of God (Isaiah 14:12-14). On Earth, in the person of Absalom, the same pattern occurred. A son, who was trusted and deeply loved by his father, turned and sought— through satanic inspiration— the usurpation of the throne.

During the time Jesus walked the earth, the pattern emerged again. This time the traitor was Judas, one of the original disciples (John 13:2,3). The repetition of Satan's behavior makes the pattern clear. The Antichrist will arise from one who has been given great trust and power. It may come from one who is even now considered a Christian, or perhaps someone of Jewish descent, or even a Muslim.

But just as God had Lucifer outflanked before, He still has all things under control. All these events are taking place in order to prove and test the people the Lord God has called unto Himself.

## Chapter Thirty-Seven

# Who can go to War Against the Beast?

Now that we observed the depth of the prophecy of the "deep state" in the Beast and the False Prophet and its outward manifestation and release on the Earth what are we to do?

Equipped with a mountaintop perspective on how the forces of darkness operate behind the scenes on Earth, the knowledge must be sealed in our hearts and minds.

When Jesus redefined His people as the real temple of God, it changed everything. No longer should God's people see themselves as mere men. His followers are radically different then the multitudes. They have a special ability to see far off.

In light of Christ's redefinition, it therefore becomes paramount to guard against being sucked back into the world's vacuum.

The spiritual void in the outside world is like a magnet which can draw a person backward. The pervasive pull can cause the loss of the new objective perspective. This is a rampant problem, as many unsuspecting souls have thus become fixated and neutralized by politics.

The contradictory powers have a brilliance of dark intelligence that can act like a spiritual quicksand.

**Observation Over Time**

The evidence becomes observable on a macro level as the tracks of the Beast have left its footprints in the annals of history. This has been demonstrated in the revelation of the Beast.

Likewise in this hour (the last one hundred years), the footprints of the False Prophet have also surfaced and become visible.

While there are a few great men, who have been called to fight the Beast and the False Prophet mano a mano in the sewer of political corruption, at best it is putting a shoulder against a bursting dam. They are the last vestige holding back the unrelenting powerful force moving the world toward a New World Order. The godless void in the outer world has been filled with a malignant energy that can only be destroyed by the return of Christ.

In the meantime, while the Lord's people wait for His return we must remember, faith cannot rest. But as the world is passing away the future is very wonderful and bright for God's people.

> "See to it that you do not refuse Him who speaks. For if the people did not escape when they refused who warned them on earth, how much less will we escape if we reject Him who warns from heaven." (Heb.12:25)

And this is a daily call. "Behold, this is the law of the house" And we are that house."There must be a continual daily exercise of faith. We simply must choose.

**The Universal Test Cannot Be Avoided**

The universal trial is coming over the entire world and is affecting everyone on the planet. Not since Abraham Lincoln, John F. Kennedy and Ronald Reagan has any president resisted the False Prophet's deep state. That was, until Donald Trump was elected. He became an enormous irritant and resistant to the globalists. His presidency became an interruption and frustration to the momentum of globalization. His administration, in that regard, is prophetic and historic!

**In Conclusion**

What has been revealed in this treatise is the prophecy of the deep state described in biblical terms as the Beast and the False prophet. This was the forewarned dark day that would come over the whole earth. And it is! The machinations taking place globally are essentially, in a figure of speech, the outer court being trampled down by the gentiles.

What we are witnessing on a grand global scale is an unprecedented world-wide test. But as the fire in the world has been heated up, we can't afford to lose focus peering into the fire. If time is wasted and invested poorly trying to fix the unfixable, the resultant effect is a diminishing of the spectacular purpose of the upward call of God in Christ Jesus.

Keep your garment clean. And, as much as possible, stay out of the outer court where carnal men trample down the world.

Keep looking up.

For the mystery of the ages is great, "Christ in YOU, the hope of glory."

## Summary

This book has shed new light on an age-old topic. It has laid out the panorama of human history so that the reader can gain greater objectivity with a fresh and clear Christian worldview. It has been shown that throughout time the human race has been moving toward a One World Government, eventually to be ruled by a man who would claim to be the master of the human race: the Antichrist.

Step by step, light has been shed on the world empires and the powerful people that have arisen throughout time and are nudging the master plan along. With the death blow to the British Empire from the great world wars of the twentieth century, the focus of this exposition shifted the spotlight onto the infamous False Prophet.

Since most theologians have been blinded by an incomplete understanding of the False Prophet, the central thesis of this book has been to identify the False Prophet and his two horns as the United States and Great Britain. It also made clear that the False Prophet has immense power(s), which he uses to set up the final system (the Beast) with ten kings. The ten kings of the Beast system shall be ruled by the coming Antichrist and have worldwide impact.

The spiritual purpose underlying this book is to retrieve and reactivate many believers who have succumbed to the temptations of the world and have lost their zeal for the Lord.

The high ground of a Christian worldview gives God's panoramic perspective on human history. When God spoke to the apostle John he was invited to come up "hither." What the invitation suggested is that John was offered to see things from God's point of view. As we are able to see with greater objectivity, it become clear that we are not of this world.

There is a new day on the horizon!

# Endnotes


**Chapter 4: Instruments of Darkness**

1. Eustace Muffins, The Secrets of the Federal Reserve (Stauton, VA: Bankers Research Institute, 1985), 3.
2. Ibid.
3. Hal Lindsey, Late Great Planet Earth (Grand Rapids: Zondervan, 1970), 105.

**Chapter 10: City of Harlots**

1. The Jewish Encyclopedia, 9:309.
2. Alexander Hislop, The Two Babylons (Neptune, NJ: Loizeaux Brothers, 1916), 40-42.
3. Ibid., 75.
4. Ibid.
5. Ibid.
6. R. Woodrow, Babylon Mystery Religion, 153.

**Chapter 11: Tracks in the Sands of Time**

1. Philip Myers, Ancient History, Table of Contents. Myers' book is a good example of many historical books that explain the evolution of the great empires.

**Chapter 12: Nimrod of the Ancient World**

1. Hislop, The Two Babylons, 41-45.
2. Ibid.
3. Ibid.
4. Ibid., 18-19.

5. Ibid., 12-19.
6. Ibid.
7. Ibid., 20-21.
8. Ibid.
9. Ibid.
10. Ibid. 41-45.
11. Ibid., 30-32.
12. Ibid.
13. Ibid.


**Chapter 13: Five Kingdoms that Fell**


1. World Book Encyclopedia (World Book Inc.: 1988), Egypt, 6:133-144.
2. Ibid.
3. Ibid.
4. Ibid.
5. Ibid.
6. Hislop, The Two Babylons, 22.
7. Ibid., 38
8. Myers, Ancient History, 62-69.
9. Ibid.
10. Ibid., 38.
11. New Bible Dictionary (Grand Rapids: Eerdmans, 1967), 119.
12. Myers, Ancient History, 88.
13. Ibid., 93-94.
14. Ibid., 89.
15. John Walvoord, Daniel—The Key to Prophetic Revelation (Chicago: Moody Press, 1971), 129-131.
16. Myers, Ancient History, 90-91.
17. Ibid., 95-97

18. Star, History of the Ancient World, 378-385.
19. Hislop, The Two Babylons, 49-50.
20. Ibid.
21. Ibid.,48.

**Chapter 14: Rome: The Sixth Empire**

1. Harper's Dictionary of Classical Literature, 1387.
2. Star, History of the Ancient World, 575.
3. Ibid., 576.
4. Ibid., 576-600.

**Chapter 15: The Seventh Head**

1. World Book, Vol. 2, the entire section on England.
2. John Reeves, The Rothschilds, Financial Rulers of the Nations, 167.
3. World Book, section on England
4. Ibid.
5. Des Griffin, Descent into Slavery (Clackamas, OR: Emissary Publications, 1978), 26-27.
6. Des Griffin, Fourth Reich of the Rich (Clackamas, OR: Emissary Publications, 1976), 41-45.
7. Ibid.
8. Anton Chaitkin, Treason in America (New York: New Benjamin Franklin House, 1985), 265-304.
9. Ibid.
10. Ibid.
11. Ibid.
12. Ibid.
13. Ibid.
14. Ibid.
15. Ibid.
16. Ibid.

17. Ibid.
18. Ibid.
19. Ibid.
20. Ibid.
21. Ibid.
22. Ibid.
23. Griffin, Descent into Slavery, 26.
24. Nesta Webster, The French Revolution (Nesta Webster, 1919), 2-36.
25. Ibid.
26. Ibid.
27. Griffin, Descent into Slavery, 26.
28. R.E. Epperson, The Unseen Hand (Tucson: Publius Press, 1985), 140.
29. Ibid.
30. Ibid.
31. Ibid.
32. Griffin, Fourth Reich of the Rich, 88.
33. Epperson, The Unseen Hand, 166 & 168.


**Chapter 18: World Wars I and II**


1. John Robinson, Proofs of Conspiracy (Boston: Western Islands, originally published in 1798), 57-156.
2. Challenging Years, 189-197.
3. Griffin, Descent into Slavery, 95-98.
4. Griffin, Fourth Reich of the Rich, 124.
5. Griffin, Descent into Slavery, 26-40.
6. Ibid.
7. Ibid.
8. Konrad Heiden, Der Fuehrer (Boston: Houghton Mifflin, 1944), 64-65.

9. Ibid., 5.
10. A.S. Sutton, Wall Street and the Rise of Hitler (Seal Beach, CA: 76 Press, 1976). The entire book is a record of the banking powers' arming of Hitler.

**Chapter 19: The Great Sword**

1. Sutton, Wall Street and the Rise of Hitler, 67-76.
2. Joseph Carr, The Twisted Cross (Shreveport, LA: Huntington House, 1985), 36.
3. Heiden, Der Fuehrer, 1-18.
4. Cleon Skousen, The Naked Capitalist (Salt Lake City: 1970), 30. Lord Balfour worked within the Round Table's elite, including both Rhodes and Rothschild.
5. Heiden, Der Fuehrer, 65.
6. Ibid., 64.
7. Ibid., 528.
8. Ibid., 586-87.

**Chapter 20: The Satanic Resurrection**

1. Griffin, Descent into Slavery, 34-46.
2. Mullins, The Secrets of the Federal Reserve, 1-2.

**Chapter 22: The False Prophet (the Second Beast)**

1. W.E. Vines, Expository Dictionary of New Testament Words (London: Oliphant, 1940, Distributed by Revel), 1:222.
2. W.E. Vines, Expository Dictionary of New Testament Words, 1:89.

**Chapter 23: The New Zion**

1. Peter Marshall, The Light and the Glory (Old Tappan, NJ: Revell, 1977), 106.
2. Ibid.

3. Ibid., 110-11.
4. Ibid.
5. Ibid.
6. Ibid.
7. Ibid.
8. Ibid.
9. Ibid., 270-309.
10. Charles Noburn, Honest Money (Asheville, NC: New Puritan Library, 1983), 8-9.
11. Ibid., 9-11.
12. Ibid.
13. Charles Norburn, Honest Government (Asheville, N.C.: New Puritan Library, 1984), 10-11.
14. Norburn, Honest Money, 10-11.
15. Ibid.
16. Ibid.
17. Skousen, Naked Capitalist, 8-11.
18. Ibid.
19. Ibid.
20. Ibid.
21. Martin Larson, The Secrets of the Federal Reserve, 10.
22. Robinson, Proofs of Conspiracy, 57-156.
23. Ibid., 58-60.
24. Ibid.
25. Ibid., 58.
26. Ibid.
27. R.E. Epperson, The New World Order (Tucson: Publius Press, 1990), 110.
28. Ibid., 84
29. Karl Marx and Frederick Engels, The Communist Manifesto (NY: International Publishers, 1948), Point #5,30.

30. Chaitken, Treason in America, 53.
31. Ibid., 5-19.
32. Ibid.
33. Ibid.
34. Ibid.
35. Ibid.
36. James D. Horan, Confederate Agent, A Discovery in History, 16.
37. William Mcllhany II, {Clandestine, 12.
38. Epperson, The Unseen Hand, 155.
39. Abraham Lincoln, speech in Springfield, IL, January 1837.
40. Epperson, The Unseen Hand, 160. The Knights of the Golden Circle was the fountainhead of the assassination.


**Chapter 24: The Post-Civil War Era**


1. G.G. McGreer, The Conquest of Poverty, 169.
2. Irwin Ungar, The Greenback Era, 1865-1869, 352-3,356-61, 370.
3. Ibid.
4. Alexander Del Mar, History of Money in America, 36.
5. Chaitkin, Treason in America, 291-304.
6. Ibid.
7. Ibid.
8. Ibid.
9. Ungar, The Greenback Era, 352-3, 356-61, 370.
10. Ibid.
11. Norburn, Honest Money, 29-35.
12. Griffin, Fourth Reich of the Rich, 88.
13. Norburn, Honest Money, 33.
14. H.S. Kenan, The Federal Reserve Bank; the Most Fantastic and Unbelievable Fraud in History (Los Angeles: The

Noontide Press, 1966, rev. 1967), 48.
15. Mullins, The Secrets of the Federal Reserve, 16.
16. Robinson, Proofs of Conspiracy. George Washington made this famous statement in response to the notion of a central bank controlled by an elite group of men.
17. Constitution of the United States of America. POWERS OF CONGRESS: Article 1, Section 8, Paragraph 5.

**Chapter 25: History of the False Prophet—Anglo-Americanism**

1. Clarence Kelly, Conspiracy Against God and Man (Belmont, MA: Western Islands, 1974). The whole book is a historical record of the conspiracy.
2. Skousen, The Naked Capitalist, 27-29.
3. Carroll Quigley, Tragedy and Hope; A History of the World in Our Times, 270-268.
4. Ibid., 130.
5. Ibid.
6. Carroll Quigley, The Anglo-American Establishment (Books in Focus, 1981), 33-34.
7. Skousen, The Naked Capitalist, 31.
8. Ibid.
9. The World Crisis: The Aftermath, 147.
10. Quigley, Tragedy and Hope, 132-133.
11. Ibid., 951.
12. Lawrence Shoup and William Minter, The Imperial Brain Trust (NY: Monthly Review Press, 1977), 1-56.
13. Phoebe Courtney, The CFR, 36.
14. Skousen, The Naked Capitalist, 31.
15. Ibid.
16. Ibid.

17. The Review of the News, April 9,1980, 37-38.
18. Skousen, The Naked Capitalist, 54.
19. Ibid.
20. Ibid., 54.

**Chapter 26: The Two-horned Beast**

1. Quigley, The Anglo-American Establishment, 3-14.
2. Sheldon Emry, Billions for Bankers, Debts for the People: How Did it Happen? (Phoenix: America's Promise Radio, 1967).
3. Ibid.
4. Chaitking, Treason in America, 293-295.
5. Griffin, Descent into Slavery, 66.
6. Ibid.
7. Kelly, Conspiracy Against God and Man, 173.

**Chapter 29: The Image of the Beast**

1. Vines, Expository Dictionary of New Testament Words, 2:243-4.
2. Ibid., 4:325-6.
3. Ibid., 2:337 & 1:149.
4. George Gurben, Annenburg School of Communication.
5. Ibid.
6. TV, The Media, 72-73.
7. Ibid.
8. Ibid.

**Chapter 32: Laser Scanning Systems for Supermarket Automation**

1. Roger Palmer, The Bar Code Book (Heleners Pub. Co., 1989), 11-14. Also, for complete history on bar code, consult Reading Between the Lines, by Craig Harmon and Russ

Adams (Heleners Pul. Co., 1984).

2. Ibid., 19.
3. Ibid.
4. Ibid.
5. Ibid., 22.
6. Mary Stewart Relfe, The New Money System (Montgomery, AL: Ministry Inc., 1981), 54.
7. Ibid., 47-53.

## Bibliography

Barnes, H.F. Pearl Harbor a Quarter Century Later. Clackamas, OR: Emissary Publications, 1968.

Boer, H.R. A Short History of the Church. Grand Rapids: Eerdmans, 1976.

Carr, J.J. The Twisted Cross. Shreveport: Huntington House, 1985.

Chaitkin, A. Treason in America. NY: New Benjamin Franklin House, 1985.

Commanger, H.S. Documents of American History. NY: Appleton, 1949.

Courtney, P., The CFR.

Del Mar, A. History of Money in America.

DeMoss, A. The Rebirth of America, U.S.A.: DeMoss, 1986.

Douglas, J.D. Red Cocaine. Atlanta: Clarion House, 1990.

Epperson, R.E. The New World Order. Tucson: Publius Press, 1990.

The Unseen Hand. Tucson: Publius Press, 1985.

Fry, L. Waters Flowing Eastward. New Orleans: Flanders Hall, 1988.

Griffin, D. Fourth Reich of the Rich. Clackamas, OR: Emissary Publications, 1976.

. Descent into Slavery. Clackamas, OR: Emissary Publications, 1978.

Heiden, C. Der Fuehrer. Boston: Houghton Mifflin, 1944.

Hislop, A. The Two Babylons. Neptune, NJ: Loizeaux Brothers, 1916.

Horan, James D. Confederate Agent; A Discovery in History.

Hunt, D. Peace, Prosperity and the Coming Holocaust. Eugene, OR: Harvest House, 1983.

Kelly, C. Conspiracy Against God and Man. Belmont, MA: Western Islands, 1974.

Kenan, H.S. The Federal Reserve Bank; the Most Fantastic and Unbelievable Fraud in History. Los Angeles: The Noontide Press, 1966 (rev. 1967).

Larson, M. The Federal Reserve.

Lindsey, H. The Late Great Planet Earth. Grand Rapids: Zondervan, 1970.

McGreer, G.G. The Conquest of Poverty.

Mcllhany, William. Klandestine.

Marrs, T. Millennium. Austin, TX: Living Truth Publishers, 1990.

Marshall, P. The Light and the Glory, Old Tappan, NJ: Fleming H. Revell, 1977.

Marx, K. and Engels, F. The Communist Manifesto. NY: International Publishers, 1948. Mullins, E. The Secrets of the Federal Reserve. Stauton, VA: Bankers Research Institute, 1985.

Myers, P. Ancient History.

New American Standard Bible, Open Bible Edition. Camden, NJ: Nelson, 1979.

Norburn, C.S. Honest Money. Ashville, NC: New Puritan Library, 1983.

Honest Government. Ashville, NC: New Puritan Library, 1984.

Palmer, R. The Bar Code Book. Helmers Pub., 1989.

Pike, W.P. Israel: Our Duty, Our Dilemma. Clackamas, OR: Emissary Publications,

1984.
Quigley, C. The Anglo-American Establishment. Books in Focus, 1981.
Tragedy and Hope: A History of the World in Our Times.
Reeves, J. The Rothschilds: Financial Rulers of the Nations.
Relfe, M.S. The New Money System.
Robertson, P. The New World Order. Word, 1991.
Robinson, J. Proofs of a Conspiracy. Boston: Western Islands.
Roebuck, C. The World of Ancient Times. 1966.
Shoup, L. and Minter, W. The Imperial Brain Trust. NY: Monthly Review Press, 1977.
Skousen, C. The Naked Capitalist. Salt Lake City: 1970.
Star, R. History of the Ancient World. NY: Oxford Press, 1974.
Stewart, M. New Money or None.
Stormer, J. None Dare Call it Treason. Florissant, Missouri Liberty Bell Press, 1964.
Sutton, A.S. Wall Street and the Rise of Hitler. Seal Beach, CA: 76 Press, 1976.
Ungar, I. The Greenback Era, 1865-1869.
Walvord, J. The Rapture Question. Grand Rapids: Zondervan, 1976.
Daniel—The Key to Prophetic Revelation. Chicago: Moody Press, 1971.
Walvord, J. The Revelation of Jesus Christ. Chicago: Moody Press, 1966.
Webster, N. Surrender of an Empire. London: Emissary Publications, 1931.
The French Revolution. N. Webster, 1919.
Woodrow, R. Babylon Mystery Religion. 1966.

# Index

## Symbols



## A



## B

## F



## G



## H

## I



## J



## L

## M



## N



## O



## P

## Q



## R



## S



## T

## About the Author

Ken Klein is a Hebrew Christian and has been a believer for more than fifty years. Ken Klein was born in Los Angeles California in 1946. He was raised in a Jewish family but his Aunt Jenny baptised him before he reached the age of one year. As a result of that baptism God's hand has been upon him for nearly his whole life. He has been married to Jan Klein for over 45 years and has three children: Jonathan, Michael, and Daniel.

At the age of eighteen Ken moved to Oregon where he starred as defensive halfback for the University of Oregon football team, and later graduated with a B.S. degree in social sciences.

After college he made his way into the National Football League briefly with both San Francisco Forty-niners in 1967 and the Houston Oilers in 1968. Two devastating injuries cut short a promising career. Ken attributes the injuries to God's providential intervention.

He has pastored three churches, authored a number of books and has produced a number of films. He has appeared on thousands of radio and television talk shows including appearances with almost every major Christian broadcaster in the United States.

He currently is executive director of Ken Klein Productions, a Christian film production company.

He has produced many video documentaries and his current films include: Temple Mount Dilemma, Petra—Israel's Secret Hiding Place, and Twenty-five Messianic Signs. The blockbuster films of Cracking the Prophetic Code (the United States in Prophecy) In the Shadow of Babylon are in strong demand. His film "Touring Israel" has been shown on numerous television stations over the years.

He has also completed a film series on the Great Pyramid, as well as Invasion of the Dark Stars, Transhumanism and His latest film Jerusalem and the Lost Temple of the Jews.

Mr. Klein can be contacted via e-mail at:

kbklein28@gmail.com

Please feel free to visit the web site at: www.kenkleinproductions.net and also www.kenkleinuniversity.com